Review Of
Financial Regulations
In The Crown Dependencies

Part Four

Isle of Man

Presented to Parliament by the Secretary of State for the Home Department

by Command of Her Majesty.

November 1998.

Cm 4109–IV

£11.40

ISLE OF MAN

A GUIDE TO

THE INTERNATIONAL FINANCE CENTRE

PART 4 OF THE REVIEW OF
FINANCIAL REGULATION IN THE CROWN DEPENDENCIES

Chief Secretary's Office

November 1998

A GUIDE TO THE INTERNATIONAL FINANCE CENTRE

CHAPTER 1

SITUATION, AREA AND POPULATION

1.1 Introduction

The Isle of Man occupies a central position, not only in the Irish Sea, but also in the British Isles. The Island is some 33 miles (52 kilometres) long from north to south and 13 miles (22 km) wide from east to west at the widest point.

The coastline, which is over 100 miles (160 km) long, encompasses an area of 227 square miles (572 sq. km.). A range of hills stretches obliquely across the Island, the highest point being Snaefell at 2,036 feet (621 metres). Around the Island's flat northern plain are long sandy beaches which contrast markedly with the rocky cliffs and sheltered bays around the rest of the coastline. Over two thirds of the land mass is cultivated, principally the fertile northern and southern plains.

1.2 Population

The Island's population is estimated at 73,100 (71,714 at the 1996 Census). The population is in natural decline, i.e. deaths exceed births, but this is more than offset by net immigration and the population has increased by some 11,200 over the last 20 years. In the last 10 to 12 years in particular, immigration has been mainly by economically active younger persons. As a consequence, the age profile of the population, which was a particular problem a decade ago, has improved significantly.

The population of the Island is similar in number to the two main Channel Islands. However, the Isle of Man is five times larger in area than Jersey and nine times larger than Guernsey, with the result that population density is much lower. The Island's population density is about half of that of the United Kingdom.

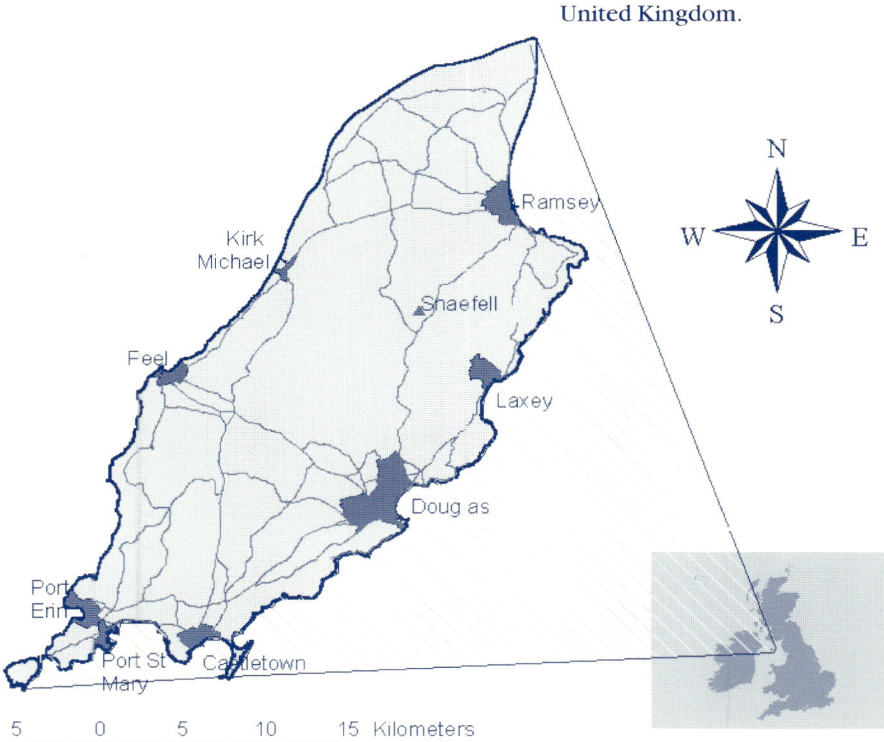

Chapter 2

Constitution, law and justice

2.1 Constitutional Background

The Isle of Man first came under the English Crown in the fourteenth century following periods under the suzerainty of the Kings of Norway and Scotland. In 1405, the Island, with its "regalities" was granted by the Crown to Sir John Stanley and his heirs. From then, up to 1765, it was ruled by the Stanleys, the Earls of Derby and later the Dukes of Athol as Kings or Lords of Man. By Acts of Parliament passed in that year and in 1825, the rights of the Lords of Man were revested in the Crown and, for a time, the Island was very largely governed from London.

The Crown

The modern constitutional relationship between the British Crown and the Island dates from 1866 when an Act of Parliament was passed separating Manx revenues from those of the United Kingdom and giving the Island a limited measure of control over insular expenditure. Since then, a long series of measures, particularly over the last 40 years, has transferred control more and more into local hands. The Island remains a Crown Dependency but is now largely self-governing.

The Crown retains responsibility for the Island's defence and external relations (for which the Island makes an annual payment to the United Kingdom Government) and has ultimate responsibility for the good government of the Island. Westminster is empowered to legislate for the Island but, by convention, does not do so without the consent of the insular authorities. Primary legislation passed by the Island's own Parliament requires the Royal Assent before it can be given effect and the Crown appoints a Lieutenant Governor, two Deemsters (Judges) and the Island's Attorney General.

The Crown acts in Island affairs on the advice of the Privy Council with the Home Secretary having particular responsibility for tendering advice. Official communications between the Island and the United Kingdom Government are channelled through the Home Office.

The European Union

The Island has a special relationship with the European Union (EU) based on Protocol 3 of the Treaty of Accession by which the United Kingdom joined the European Communities. It is a limited relationship which is confined to ensuring free movement of goods and agricultural products and conformity with EU customs arrangements. The Island neither contributes to, nor receives support from, the EU Budget.

International Agreements

Any treaty or international agreement to which the United Kingdom Government becomes a party is not considered as applying automatically to the Island. Any such treaty or agreement may, however, expressly be applied to the Island, following consultation with the Island.

2.2 Insular Administration

Tynwald

The Island's Parliament, known as Tynwald, has a long history traceable back over a thousand years and has a long and strong democratic tradition which includes giving votes to women in 1881, well before England

and Wales. It does not derive its legislative competence from any grant from the Crown, or from any grant of authority by the Parliament at Westminster. Tynwald was and is a Parliament of an ancient Kingdom. It comprises two Branches. These are the House of Keys (24 Members, popularly elected), and the Legislative Council (11 Members, all but two of whom are elected by the House of Keys, the others being the Lord Bishop and the Attorney General). These Chambers sit separately in public and each considers primary legislation. The Keys and the Council sit together in public in a third Chamber, Tynwald, to debate policy, to consider secondary legislation and to vote monies.

The procedure for passing primary legislation (an Act of Tynwald) is very similar to that of the Westminster Parliament. Each Branch will give a Bill three readings. Bills are treated as passed when they receive the Royal Assent and that Assent is announced in Tynwald.

Government policy and finances are subjected to scrutiny and endorsement by Tynwald through an annual Policy Document considered each October and a Budget considered each March. This bi-annual scrutiny process provides a "rolling accountability" which suits a political environment from which political parties are largely absent.

A register of the interests of Members of Tynwald is maintained in which Members are required to record their interests comprehensively, including all directorships, employments, pecuniary interests, shareholdings and investments. Members are not appointed to Departments of Government where their private interests would conflict with the responsibilities of the Department. In the case of an occasional conflict of interest, this is declared and the Member takes no part in the relevant decision-making process.

LEGISLATURE

Parliament:	Tynwald, comprising Lower House - House of Keys Upper House - Legislative Council	
Members:	House of Keys	24
	Legislative Council	11
Electoral System:	House of Keys - constituency elections by simple majority Legislative Council - 9 elected by the House of Keys 2 ex officio	
President of Tynwald:	The Hon Sir Charles Kerruish, OBE, LLD(hc), CP	
Speaker of the House of Keys:	The Hon. Noel Q. Cringle, SHK	

The Executive

Government is by a Ministerial system introduced in 1987. There is a Chief Minister, elected by Tynwald. The Chief Minister, in turn, nominates 9 Ministers to be responsible for the 9 Departments of Government and the Chief Minister and the 9 Ministers serve as a Council of Ministers - in effect, a Cabinet. The Treasury is the Department with a particular responsibility for the Financial Services Sector.

The Treasury is headed by a Minister and three other Members of Tynwald. They are not expected to hold any non-executive directorships which could conflict with their responsibilities to the Treasury. Where there is a potential for private interests to be material and relevant to the Department's responsibilities, those interests are declared and minuted. Members then refrain from taking part in any consideration of such matters.

The Treasury has a permanent establishment of 302 full-time civil servants, allocated between different divisions as follows:

	Full-time equivalents
Administration	6
International Services	7
Customs and Excise	44
Economic Affairs	10
Finance	55
Income Tax	114
Information Systems	56
Internal Audit	10
	302

The Customs and Excise Division includes an Intelligence and Investigation Section which employs 7 staff. These work closely with the Police Fraud Squad. The possibility of establishing a Joint Financial Investigation and Enforcement Unit is under active consideration.

The two principal regulating bodies of the Financial Services Sector are the Financial Supervision Commission and the Insurance and Pensions Authority (see Section 5.3). Both are Statutory Boards which report to the Council of Ministers through the Treasury and each is chaired by a Member of the Treasury.

EXECUTIVE

Council of Ministers:	Chief Minister and 9 Ministers
Departments of Government:	Department of Agriculture, Fisheries and Forestry Department of Education Department of Health and Social Security Department of Home Affairs Department of Local Government and the Environment Department of Tourism and Leisure Department of Trade and Industry Department of Transport Department of the Treasury
Chief Minister:	Hon. D.J. Gelling, FInstSMM, FIMgt, MHK
Chief Secretary:	Mr. J.F. Kissack, B. Com., FIMgt.

2.3 Legal System and Legislation

The Isle of Man is an entirely separate legal jurisdiction to the United Kingdom. It is not part of the realm of England nor is it governed by the laws of England.

However, the system of law which exists in the Isle of Man is a common law system similar to that which exists in England. During recent centuries, the Manx Courts have generally followed English precedents, unless there was some provision in Manx law to the contrary. English precedents are not binding, but are treated as highly persuasive. The Isle of Man has, in practice, become an English common law country by adoption.

On many subjects, a conscious effort has been, and is, made to keep Manx law in line with English law. This is certainly the case with criminal law, contract, tort, regulation of the financial services industry and many aspects of commercial law.

Government legislation is introduced in accordance with a rolling three year programme, revised annually, and approved by the Council of Ministers. Government Bills are drafted in the Chambers of the Island's Attorney General on the instructions of the Council of Ministers. Two Legislative Draftsmen are employed for this purpose and they are supported by library, administrative and secretarial officers within the Chambers. The Draftsmen are able to call upon the expertise of other legal staff in the Chambers.

The principal legislation relating to financial regulation, fraud and money laundering is listed with brief annotations in the annex. The legislation on the investigation of crime and the pursuit of the proceeds of crime follows closely that of the United Kingdom.

2.4 Judicial System

The Judicial System of the Isle of Man is recognisably similar to that in the United Kingdom. There are two permanent Judges, the First and Second Deemsters, titles which derive from the 13th Century, if not earlier. The Deemsters are appointed by the Crown after consultation with the Island's Authorities. The Governor has the power to appoint acting Deemsters of the High Court, a power which is exercised for cases of unusual length or requiring particular expertise. In addition, there are two full-time stipendiary magistrates known as the High Bailiff and the Deputy High Bailiff, who deal principally with summary offences.

Civil matters are usually heard at first instance by a single Deemster sitting in the High Court. Criminal proceedings are heard at first instance before one of the stipendiary magistrates or a bench of lay Magistrates, in less serious cases. More serious cases are heard before a Deemster sitting with a Jury of seven in the Court of General Gaol Delivery, the equivalent of the English Crown Court. All criminal cases are dealt with in the same way and there is no special procedure for financial or fiscal cases.

Civil and criminal appeals are dealt with by an Appeal Court which is known as the Staff of Government Division. Appeals are usually heard by a Deemster and a Judge of Appeal who is chosen from prominent members of the English Bar. The Judge of Appeal is appointed by the Crown on the advice of the Home Secretary in London. A Deemster is not permitted to hear appeals against his own decisions.

Where important points of law are at stake, there is a further avenue of appeal to the Judicial Committee of the Privy Council in London.

The Deemsters do not sit as part of Tynwald and the Island's judiciary is independent of the legislature and executive. When the Lieutenant Governor is absent from the Isle of Man, the First Deemster performs the role of Acting Governor. Apart from this occasional duty, the First Deemster has no other official role within the legislature or the executive.

JUDICIARY	
First Deemster appointed by the Crown:	Deemster T.W Cain
Second Deemster appointed by the Crown:	Deemster J.M. Kerruish
High Bailiff appointed by the Lieutenant Governor:	A.K. Williamson
Deputy High Bailiff appointed by the Lieutenant Governor:	T. M. Moyle

2.5 Prosecution System

The Isle of Man does not have a Crown Prosecution Service similar to that in England and Wales. Prosecutions in Courts of Summary Jurisdiction and in committal hearings are usually conducted by a Police Officer, the system being similar to that in place in many areas of England and Wales before the creation of the Crown Prosecution Service. More complex or serious cases before Courts of Summary Jurisdiction are dealt with by legal officers in the Attorney General's Chambers and it is a common occurrence for the Police to seek advice from the Attorney General's Chambers on relevant legal points.

When appropriate, civil proceedings and/or prosecutions can be brought in the name of either the Insurance and Pensions Authority or the Financial Supervision Commission. These cases will involve breaches of the relevant regulatory legislation.

All proceedings before a Deemster and jury in the Court of General Gaol Delivery are conducted in the name of the Attorney General by Legal Officers in the Attorney General's Chambers.

Decisions to prosecute in the Summary Courts are made by the prosecutor (usually the Police).

Proceedings before the Court of General Gaol Delivery are instituted by a document known as an Information which is signed by the Attorney General. That document is, to all intents and purposes, identical to an Indictment under English law.

The office of Attorney General combines the functions of the English Attorney General, the Director of Public Prosecutions and the Director of the Serious Fraud Office. The Attorney General is appointed by the Crown on the advice of the Secretary of State after consulting the Island's Authorities and his first responsibility is to the Crown. As a Crown appointment, the Attorney General is able to take an independent view in relation to criminal proceedings and criminal policy matters. The office-holder is an ex-officio non-voting member of the Legislative Council and attends meetings of the Council of Ministers as legal adviser. The independent position of the Attorney General is illustrated by the fact that he can be called upon to give advice on Manx law to both the Crown and the Island's Authorities.

The policy of the Attorney General is to commence proceedings if there is sufficient evidence to warrant a prosecution and there is a realistic prospect of conviction; proceedings will, subject to accepted criminal policy considerations, then be commenced.

The independence of the Attorney General is further evidenced by the fact that prosecutions have been mounted as appropriate against Departments of Government. The principles which apply to decisions to prosecute in the Isle of Man are, in effect, the same as those applied in England and Wales. Political or commercial pressures do not impinge upon the decision of the Attorney General, Police or Regulatory Authorities in deciding whether to prosecute.

All classes of criminal case, whether they be financial, administrative or other crimes, are subject to the same procedures and considerations in determining whether to prosecute and in the conduct of court proceedings. There is no class of financial crime in respect of which procedures are different to those in other criminal cases.

The Attorney General has the power, as does the English Attorney General, to grant, in effect, immunity from prosecution. There is no general immunity granted in respect of any class of offence and the grant of immunity in any particular case is very rare and requires quite exceptional circumstances.

PUBLIC PROSECUTORS	
Attorney General appointed by the Crown:	Mr. W.J.H. Corlett
Government Advocate:	Mr. A.T.K. Corlett

CHAPTER 3

ECONOMY AND FINANCE INDUSTRY

3.1 The Economy

The Isle of Man Government's core policy in relation to the economy is:

> *"to pursue manageable and sustainable growth based on a diversified economy with the aims of.*
>
> *(a) raising the standard of living of the whole population;*
>
> *(b) securing continuous future prosperity throughout the Island; and*
>
> *(c) providing the resources needed to sustain public services."*

Historically, the Island's economy was based on tourism and agriculture. The relative decline of these industries over the last 35 years has required the Island to diversify and, whilst agriculture and tourism continue to make their contribution, the economy is now led by financial services (37% of GDP) and manufacturing (10% of GDP). National Income is increasing steadily but remains comparatively modest, with GDP per head, being some 79% of average United Kingdom levels (latest figures for 1995/96).

The cost of living in the Island is substantially the same as that in the United Kingdom. Prices of imported goods and energy costs tend to be higher but these are offset by, in particular, lower housing and related costs.

The Island is in currency union with the United Kingdom, although the Island issues its own currency which is legal tender only within the Island. Interest rates are, therefore, similar to those applying in the United Kingdom and the rate of inflation changes broadly in line with United Kingdom movements.

The growth of the Island's economy and the comparison of the Island's GDP per head with that of the United Kingdom during 1985/86 to 1995/96 is shown in the following table:

Isle of Man Gross Domestic Product 1985/86 to 1995/96

	Isle of Man GDP (Constant Prices £000's)	*Isle of Man GDP per head as a percentage of United Kingdom*
1985/86	314,857	57
1987/88	412,125	67
1989/90	492,425	71
1991/92	521,278	77
1993/94	538,875	77
1995/96	584,442	79

The change in relative importance of the sectors of the Island's economy over the same period is shown in the following table:

Income Generated in Basic Sectors from Manx Sources 1985/86 to 1995/96 (Constant Prices)(£000's)

	1985/86	*%*	*1995/96*	*%*
Manufacturing	51,591	15	65,140	10
Finance	75,686	22	242,212	37
Tourism	40,441	12	37,887	6
Construction	30,869	9	36,498	6
Agriculture & Fisheries	9,698	3	9,548	1
Public Administration	24,021	7	36,127	5
Professional & Scientific Services	41,413	12	98,827	15
Other Services	76,611	22	131,276	20
Total	**359,329**	**100**	**657,515**	**100**

Numbers in employment in the various sectors at the time of the last Census in 1996 were as follows:

Employment in Sectors of I.O.M. Economy (1996)

		%
Agriculture, Forestry and Fishing	938	3
Manufacturing	3,562	11
Construction	3,372	10
Electricity, Gas and Water	462	1
Transport and Communications	2,688	8
Wholesale Distribution	781	2
Retail Distribution	2,911	9
Financial Services	5,942	18
Professional Services	6,081	18
Tourist Accommodation	765	2
Entertainment and Catering	1,156	3
Miscellaneous Services	2,773	8
Public Administration	2,146	6
Total	**33,577**	**100**

Note: Classifications based on main source of employment. Secondary employment is excluded.

Employment in the Financial Services Sector (1996)

		%
Banking	1,781	5
Insurance	1,657	5
Other financial institutions	1,229	4
Property	536	2
Other	739	2
Total	**5,942**	**18**

The most recent data available on employment show 36,224 persons employed (June, 1998) and 386 persons unemployed (June, 1998). The rate of unemployment in April 1998 was just 1.1%.

3.2 Public Expenditure

The Island has well-developed education, health and welfare services provided by Government and publicly funded which are broadly comparable to, and in a number of respects more generous than, the equivalent public services provided in the United Kingdom. The principal sources of finance for the net funding of these services are:

Income Taxes	£119 million per annum
Indirect Taxes	£145 million per annum
National Insurance contributions	£71 million per annum

Indirect taxation and National Insurance contributions are, for most practical purposes, the same as those in the United Kingdom. The Island has, therefore, a relatively broad tax base and the funding of Government services is not wholly dependent upon taxes on income. Taxation revenue on the Island expressed as a proportion of national income is similar to that in the United Kingdom.

The Island is statutorily required to operate a balanced budget. There is no National Debt to speak of and the Island's administration has been able to build up a modest Reserve Fund of some £128 million.

Government's net revenue expenditure, estimated for 1998/99, is £264 million. This expenditure represents some 41% of GDP. In addition, there is annual capital expenditure of nearly £40 million.

3.3 Finance Industries

Origins of the Sector

The Island's economic policy is not geared exclusively to the development of the Financial Services Sector but to the creation of a diversified economy and a wide range of businesses and industries are represented on the Island. Recent growth areas outside of financial services have been ship registration, ship management and a small, but expanding, film industry.

Although the Island has pursued diversification and has welcomed a wide range of economic developments, it is the Financial Services Sector which has provided most of the growth in recent years. Finance is now the largest sector, and has been the highest income earning primary sector of the economy since 1972. The figure of 37% of GDP understates the importance of the sector to the Island as parts of other sectors, notably professional and scientific services, act in support of the finance sector, providing legal, accountancy and other services.

The origins of the Financial Services Sector on the Island may be traced back to 1961 when certain executive powers were transferred from the Lieutenant Governor to the then Finance Board (now the Treasury). One of the first actions taken was the abolition of surtax on personal incomes. The standard rate of income tax was also reduced, in 1962, from 22.5% to 21.25%. There subsequently began to develop a professional financial services infrastructure to assist in the investment management and planning of personal wealth.

Finance, steadily growing into an important industry, was given a particular boost in 1972 with the rescheduling of the Sterling Area which restricted the holding of Sterling outside the United Kingdom. A further advancement was the abolition of exchange controls in 1979. But a deep recession in the early nineteen eighties coincided with difficulties affecting the Island's banking structure (most particularly the collapse of the Savings and Investment Bank); difficulties which were to lead to the establishment of the Financial Supervision Commission in July, 1983, and an immediate overhaul of the licensing requirements and regulatory system for deposit-taking institutions. The Commission originally regulated both deposit-taking institutions and insurance businesses and then later investment business. A separate Insurance Authority to supervise and regulate the insurance industry was established in 1986. This separate Authority has since evolved into the Insurance and Pensions Authority.

The economy recovered strongly from the mid-1980s onwards as the United Kingdom emerged from recession, as world financial markets were gradually liberalised, and as personal and corporate awareness in respect of financial methods and instruments grew. Reinforcing these favourable external factors, the Island Government embarked upon a review of its legislative and fiscal framework aimed at attracting direct investment, coinciding with marketing and promotion drives for new residents, and manufacturing and financial services investment. There were major innovations with the establishing of exempt company status initially for insurance companies (1981) but later extended (1984), the widening of the appeal of the Shipping Register (1984 and 1991), the lowering of the standard rate of personal income tax to 15% and a top rate of 20%, the extension of commercial tax allowances, provisions for managed banks, and others.

The 1980s to date have seen a gradual increase in the dominance of the financial services sector. Notable initiatives in the 1990s have included tax exemption for certain classes of partnerships, the International Business Act, a new class of collective investment scheme for professional investors, legislation for Limited Liability Companies and the facility to permit the transfer of domicile of companies.

Reasons for Business

There will be various reasons for establishing financial businesses on the Isle of Man, but there is a range of attractions which will influence individual businesses. An attractive fiscal environment is central. However, other features which are influential are:

(a) political and economic stability;

(b) reputation for quality business;

(c) established regulatory standards;

(d) English language;

(e) favourable time zone;

(f) cost-effective business environment;

(g) good external communications;

(h) broadly based and skilled professional support;

(i) Government policy conducive to economic growth;

(j) attractive quality of life;

(k) legal system based on English common law.

Individual Business Areas

The Financial Services Sector on the Island, although small in global terms, is diverse and comprises a range of compatible and inter-related business areas. These may be categorised as follows:

(a) Banks and Building Societies

There are 65 banks and 3 building societies licensed to conduct their business on the Isle of Man. The banks include the major United Kingdom clearers, as well as Irish, American, European, Indian and Middle Eastern Institutions. Between them, they employ 1,781 people.

The nature of the Island's banking business is largely deposit taking from ex-patriate and foreign depositors, in addition to a range of financial services, including fund management, in keeping with the international trend for institutions to develop diversified, multi-business banking operations. Monies are generally redeposited on an inter bank basis back to London, or the Channel Islands. In this way, Isle of Man generated business brings significant advantage to London.

The Isle of Man is not party to the EU "passporting" arrangements and therefore makes individual decisions on each licensing application received.

(b) Bureaux de Change

Licensing policy does not extend to Bureaux de Change and, therefore, the Isle of Man does not have independent Bureaux. There is one Bureau de Change office within a travel agents because it is covered by the HSBC banking licence of its parent.

(c) Collective Investment Schemes and the Fund Management Industry

The Financial Supervision Act 1988 defines two main classifications of open-ended Collective Investment Scheme which may be established in the Island. Authorised and Restricted Schemes of which there are two sub-categories - exempt restricted schemes and Professional Investor funds.

The Isle of Man is a designated territory for the purpose of the United Kingdom Financial Services Act 1988. This status was granted following an evaluation of the Isle of Man regulatory regime regarding Schemes by HM Treasury who assessed that the level of protection afforded to investors in Isle of Man authorised schemes is equivalent to that in the United Kingdom. Investments in Isle of Man authorised schemes are protected by the Authorised Collective Investment Schemes (Compensation) Regulations 1988. Qualifying Isle of Man authorised schemes are, therefore, eligible for "fast track" recognition and direct promotion to the United Kingdom general public.

Currently there are 16 authorised and 85 restricted schemes established in the Isle of Man, with 23 licensed fund managers and 5 third party fund administrators.

Funds under management by regulated entities in the authorised, restricted and exempt restricted schemes total, as at 31st March, 1998, £7.5 billion. It should be noted that other jurisdictions include in their statistics closed ended companies (investment trusts) and non local funds to which, for example, investment management or advice services are provided. Such companies, as well as Isle of Man Professional Investor Funds and exempt restricted schemes administered by non-licenceholders, are not included in the Island's statistics.

The Island is, therefore, a much more significant centre for fund management than simple statistical comparison would suggest.

(d) Investment Businesses

The Investment Business Act 1991 encompasses all investment activity relating to dealing, arranging deals, giving or offering advice to investors or potential investors or managing investments in much the same way as the Financial Services Act in the United Kingdom.

In order to address the nature of the international business, the Investment Business Act goes several steps further than the United Kingdom Act in terms of its reach. A particular feature of the Investment Business Act which is different to the Financial Services Act is that all Isle of Man incorporated companies and all foreign companies "holding out" from the Isle of Man - no matter where in the world they are carrying out their business, must be licensed by the Financial Supervision Commission if they are conducting investment business. Accordingly, the reach of the Act extends to all those engaged in investment business in, on or from the Isle of Man.

Additionally, 35 banks undertake investment business and this activity is covered by their banking licence although they are still compliance-tested by investment business specialist regulatory staff.

The final category of persons carrying out investment business are the lawyers and accountants who, in the same way as in the United Kingdom, are authorised to do so by their respective professional institutions. The Institute of Chartered Accountants in England and Wales has authorised 4 Isle of Man based firms, the Law Society of England and Wales, a further 4 and the Isle of Man Law Society, 24.

(e) Life Assurance

The Isle of Man has 15 authorised life assurance companies. These companies are incorporated and managed and controlled on the Island. The majority of them are subsidiaries of very large United Kingdom life assurance and investment groups. They provide life assurance-based investment products to international investors around the world.

The first such company was established on the Island in 1977 and the sector has grown steadily since that time. Originally, the companies sold policies predominantly to high net worth British expatriates working in the Middle and Far East but that customer base has since diversified to policyholders (British and foreign nationals) all over the world. There are now approximately 1800 people directly employed on the Island by these companies with some £7 billions of policyholders' funds under management. Annual premium income for 1997 was approximately £1.5 billion.

(f) Captive and Other Insurance

There are currently 167 captive insurance companies based on the Isle of Man. These companies are incorporated, managed and controlled on the Island. Typically, they are subsidiaries of major industrial organisations around the world and are set up as dedicated insurance vehicles to help those organisations manage their insurance and risk management programmes more efficiently. They do not employ their own staff but are usually managed on the Island by specialist firms of insurance managers. These managers tend to be subsidiaries of some of the world's largest insurance, insurance broking and risk management companies.

The first captive was established on the Island in 1981 and the market experienced particularly strong periods of growth during the mid 1980s and early 1990s when conditions in the world insurance markets were particularly conducive to the formation of captives (high commercial insurance rates and limited availability of cover for some classes). This coincided with the strengthening of the Island's insurance legislation and the creation of a supervisory framework which made it a credible international centre for insurance business.

In the early years of the Isle of Man's development as an insurance centre, the captives established tended to be subsidiaries of United Kingdom companies but, in recent times, although the United Kingdom is still a very important market for the Island, there have been captives formed by companies in many other countries. Total premium income of these companies in 1997 was approximately £900 millions.

In addition to captive insurers, the Isle of Man also has a small number of specialist general insurers and reinsurers.

The Isle of Man also has a number of branches of United Kingdom-authorised insurance companies. Most of these have been established for many years and their principal purpose is to serve the domestic market on the Isle of Man, in contrast to the international life companies and captives, whose markets and risks are overseas.

(g) Pension Schemes

The pensions market on the Isle of Man currently comprises several different parts. Firstly, there are schemes established by local and other companies to serve their Manx employees and sometimes employees working further afield. Such schemes may be insurance-based with the business written by companies locally or elsewhere (usually the United Kingdom) or may be trust-based. Secondly, there is also a substantial volume of personal pensions and retirement planning business written by the authorised life assurance companies described above or the branches of United Kingdom companies based on the Island.

A major recent initiative of the Manx Treasury, through the offices of the Insurance and Pensions Authority, involves the examination of the existing arrangements for the supervision of pensions schemes on the Isle of Man and the introduction of a regulatory regime for those areas not currently subject to regulation, to ensure the security of such arrangements both for Manx residents and members of Isle of Man pension schemes, wherever they reside and work.

A Pensions Bill is scheduled for introduction into Tynwald later this year.

(h) Other Finance Business

The Isle of Man is a major centre for company registrations and company services. The Island also has a significant trusts sector. Later Chapters give details.

3.4 Geographic Distribution of Financial Business

The Isle of Man Government has only limited information on the geographic distribution of the financial business transacted in or from the Island. The data that is available is summarised in the chart below:

Deposit taking	*Liabilities (£bn)*	*Assets (£bn)*
Non bank		
Isle of Man	4.27	0.92
Other Crown Territories	0.19	0.09
United Kingdom	4.41	0.17
Other EU countries	2.00	
North America	0.63	
Rest of the world	3.92	1.65
Total non-bank	15.42	2.83
Inter bank		
Isle of Man	1.28	0.12
Other Crown Territories	0.08	1.59
United Kingdom	0.37	10.12
Rest of the world	1.04	3.07
Total inter-bank	2.77	14.90
Other	**1.11**	**1.57**
Total	**19.30**	**19.30**

What the data do show is the role that the Island performs in channelling investment into the United Kingdom.

In addition, funds under management are estimated to exceed £16 billion, much of which is invested in, or through, the City of London.

There is in the Government's legislative programme a Statistics Bill. This Bill is to be introduced in the next legislative session and will facilitate the collection of additional economic data.

3.5 Importance of the Financial Services Sector

The Island has no significant natural physical resources beyond the wild beauty of its land and seascapes, and for much economic activity, its relative isolation and the associated transportation costs are disadvantages for businesses. As is shown by the data above, the strength of the Financial Services Sector is crucial to the economic and social welfare of the Island. It is, by a significant margin, the largest component of the Island's diversified economy, providing income, particularly from external sources, wealth and employment. Its growth is the principal reason for the influx of economically active young people, particularly qualified people of Manx origin, who have boosted the Island's population numbers and have improved the age profile of the population. Government's revenues and public services are heavily dependent on the profits and incomes generated by the Financial Services Sector.

From the United Kingdom's point of view, the Financial Services industry has an importance which goes beyond ensuring the continued viability and self sufficiency of the Island. The services provided on the Island are used by residents of the United Kingdom and by British citizens abroad. Many of the financial institutions on the Island are branches or subsidiaries of United Kingdom financial institutions so that incomes and profits are remitted to the United Kingdom. The financial services provided on and from the Island are offered world-wide and funds from around the globe are invested through Manx financial institutions. The bulk of these funds, from whatever national origin, are channelled through the City of London, helping to sustain the volume of business transacted by British institutions. Best estimates suggest that some £6 bn more funds are invested into the United Kingdom by the Island's deposit takers than are sourced from there.

The Island is also a source of employment to United Kingdom citizens as most of the immigrants into the Island are persons who sustain the growth of the financial services industry and come from the United Kingdom. The ease of movement of persons between the United Kingdom and the Isle of Man means that the Island, subject to work permit arrangements, offers job and career development opportunities to many young people from the United Kingdom interested in working in the finance industry.

Chapter 4

Taxation

4.1 Policies

Public services in the Isle of Man are financed by fees, charges, rents, admissions, etc., with the balance of cost being met by taxation income.

The Isle of Man Government, therefore, levies direct and indirect taxes on its residents and associations only at such levels as are required to finance such public services.

Under Section 9 of the Treasury Act 1985, the Government is required to budget for a surplus of receipts over payments. Other key objectives of the current Budget strategy affecting taxation policy are:

- to increase the level of operating balances
- to increase the level of the Reserve Fund to the equivalent of half of Government's annual revenue funded gross expenditure in the long term and as resources allow
- to increase personal income tax allowances at least in line with inflation
- to take and keep out of the income tax system those on modest incomes
- generally to reduce the impact of income tax from time to time
- to maintain the Customs and Excise Agreement with the United Kingdom

4.2 Indirect Taxes

The Isle of Man's indirect taxation system closely follows that of the United Kingdom. The Island has some scope for introducing minor variations but, generally, it levies value added tax and customs and excise duties at the same rates and subject to the same conditions and on the same range of goods and services as the United Kingdom. The Island maintains a Customs and Excise Agreement with Her Majesty's Government which has, in a variety of forms, been in existence for over a century. The Agreement provides both parties with benefits and enables a common customs and fiscal area to exist. There is full co-operation between the two Customs organisations to prevent abuse of the indirect tax and duty systems. Through the Agreement, the Island has access to the European Single Market and has increasingly developed investigation, intelligence and data links with the EU and its members.

4.3 Direct Taxes

The Island's income tax system was introduced in 1918. In general, persons who are resident for income tax purposes are liable to income tax on world-wide income; persons who are not resident are liable on any Manx source income. Where the Manx source income falls within either an extra statutory concession, such as approved bank and building society interest, or is covered by the double taxation arrangement with the United Kingdom, payments are made gross and no action is taken to pursue any income tax liability.

There are no capital, inheritance or withholding taxes.

Individuals

With effect from 6th April 1998, individuals who are resident are entitled to a personal allowance of £7,070. For a married couple the personal allowances are fully transferable giving a combined allowance of £14,140. In addition, relief is available for interest paid, private pension contributions and nursing expenses together with a few other deductions such as deeds of covenant for charitable donations.

After allowing for the various allowances and reliefs the remaining taxable income is charged to income tax. The first £9,500 (£19,000 for a married couple) of taxable income is charged at 15% and the balance at 20%. The high tax thresholds result in 36% of individuals paying no income tax.

Non resident individuals are not entitled to any personal allowances. Income tax at 20% is charged on any income arising in the Island other than those covered by extra statutory concession or falling within the double taxation arrangement with the United Kingdom. Where a liability does arise the Assessor will, in most cases, require the tax to be deducted at source.

Companies

(a) Resident Companies

A Manx incorporated company is deemed to be resident unless it files a non resident company declaration. That declaration can be challenged if the Assessor has reason to believe that the company is in fact resident. In such circumstances the test is the same as for any foreign incorporated company, namely where the central management and control is exercised. There is no statutory definition of central management and control and therefore case law plays an important part in determining where that is actually carried on. The practice has been to use UK case law as persuasive argument provided it does not clash with any specific legislation or rulings in the Isle of Man.

Companies which are resident in the Island for taxation purposes are, subject to any specific exemptions, liable to income tax on their worldwide income. That is to say any income which arises from any source whatsoever in or out of the Isle of Man. The calculation of the income is determined in accordance with normal accountancy provisions other than where there is a specific provision within the Income Tax Acts covering particular deductions or sources of income.

The normal basis of assessment is the income of the previous year. It has been a long standing practice to accept the twelve month account ending in the previous year as representing the income for that tax year. Special provisions exist in the opening and closing years of a source of income to enable it to be assessed on the income arising in the year.

There are no capital taxes although relief is available for approved capital expenditure such as the acquisition of plant and machinery for trading purposes. The capital allowances regime which exists in the Island is in essence the United Kingdom system in force as at 5th April 1994. The one main difference is that the Island has retained the 100% first year allowance and extended it to specific commercial activities such as agricultural buildings and industrial premises. Relief for tourist premises was introduced long before the United Kingdom legislation came into existence and therefore it is covered by separate provisions. There is a specific incentive for tourist premises which extends relief to a total of 250%.

Any dividends paid by a company are allowed as a deduction in calculating the taxable income of the company. Where the dividend is paid to a non resident the company is required to deduct non resident income tax of 20% and remit it within 14 days to the Income Tax Division.

The remaining taxable income is then charged to income tax at a rate of 20% with double taxation relief being given for any overseas income which has already suffered income tax by deduction at source or otherwise. For fund management companies there is a concessionary rate of income tax of

5% on the net fees which arise from the management of collective investment schemes, other income being charged at 20%.

Trading losses arising out of excess expenditure or capital allowances can be set off against other income or can be carried forward. Group relief provisions exist to enable such losses to be set off against the income of other group companies in a manner similar to that of the United Kingdom.

Failure to comply with the legislation can result in prosecution and/or a tax geared penalty being applied.

(b) Non-resident companies

Residence is a taxation concept and can apply to companies which are incorporated in the Isle of Man as well as to companies incorporated elsewhere. For example, a company incorporated in the United Kingdom carrying on business in the Island through a permanent establishment is a non resident company. Equally, a Manx incorporated company which is managed and controlled from outside the Island is also a non resident company.

Manx or foreign incorporated companies managed and controlled outside the Island will be liable to non resident income tax at 20% on any taxable income arising in the Island e.g. trading profits, rental income and dividends. Otherwise, Manx tax does not arise. In addition, a Manx incorporated company will be required to pay non resident company duty of £750. Experience has shown that the activities of such companies are mainly investment holding but they can include any of the normal range of activities carried on by any company anywhere in the world.

(c) Tax exempt companies

Manx and foreign incorporated companies which are resident in the Isle of Man for tax purposes may be exempted from a liability to pay income tax provided certain conditions are satisfied. From a taxation aspect the specific requirements are -

- the company does not carry on or transact any trade or business which is prescribed e.g. the manufacture or sale of goods on the Island;
- it is not carrying on a licensable activity such as banking or insurance;
- all receipts and income arise outside the Island or from other exempt companies and originate from persons who are not resident in the Island;
- no person resident in the Island has any interest in the company.

In addition to the specific tax issues there are some regulatory requirements such as the need for a resident director and a resident and qualified (or Treasury approved) company secretary. Undertakings and statutory declarations have to be supplied confirming that the provisions of the legislation will be or have been complied with.

The current fee for exempt company status, which has to be by way of annual application, is £400.

(d) Tax exempt insurance companies

A resident insurance company can be exempted from income tax on the whole or part of its profits or income provided certain conditions have been satisfied. From a purely taxation perspective, the whole or part of its underwriting profits and losses must arise solely on insurance risks undertaken by the company outside the Island (irrespective of the place of making any agreement in respect of such risks) other than for insurance business carried on with other insurance companies which have also been granted exemption.

(e) International Companies

Resident companies, irrespective of where they are incorporated, which satisfy the requirements of the International Business

Act may apply to have a rate of tax which is chargeable according to the specific requirements of the company. This can be on a sliding scale up to a maximum of 35% of taxable profits computed along normal income tax lines but subject to a minimum tax charge of £1,200. Once made and agreed, there is no provision which enables a company for that year of assessment to rescind its application or apply for a different rate of tax to be levied. The conditions which have to be met are similar to those for an exempt company.

With few exceptions the provisions of the Income Tax Acts apply e.g. filing of returns, collection of tax, employers requirements, etc. Equally, as with exempt companies, there are some regulatory requirements such as the need for a resident director and a resident and qualified (or Treasury approved) company secretary. Undertakings and declarations have to be supplied confirming that the provisions of the legislation will be or have been complied with.

(f) Limited Liability Companies

This is a hybrid entity which has its origin in America. The legislation introduced in the Isle of Man is modelled on that approved by the Internal Revenue Service for the State of Wyoming. In many ways it can be thought of as operating in a similar manner to a limited partnership, except it is incorporated like a company and thus possesses a separate legal entity from its members. In this respect it can be likened to the Scottish form of "limited partnership". It has a life limited to 30 years.

The taxation of the company is also similar to that of a partnership with the profit being allocated to its members who in turn are assessed to income tax according to their residence status (see later item on partnerships). Normal income tax principles apply to the calculation of the taxable income.

An international limited liability company may be tax exempt on a similar basis to the exempt company.

Partnerships

(a) General

For Manx tax purposes partnerships are not assessed to income tax; it is the partners of the partnership who are assessed. The taxation treatment is therefore dependent upon where the business of the partnership is carried on and where the partners are resident for tax purposes. For example -

- a partnership being carried on within the Island will give rise to local source income. A non resident partner will be liable to non resident income tax at 20% on the share of profit whilst a resident partner will be required to declare his or her share on the annual income tax return together with any other income;
- if the business is carried on wholly outside the Isle of Man normal income tax rules will apply in that it will no longer be Manx source income and only resident partners will be liable to Manx income tax on the share of profit.

(b) Limited Partnership

These are not treated any differently for tax purposes to any other partnership. A limited partner will be liable to income tax on any share of profit which arises in the Isle of Man.

(c) International Limited Partnerships

These are very similar to the exempt company in that it is exempt from income tax if it satisfies very similar criteria. There is in addition a requirement to have all the limited partners resident outside the Island although, for regulatory purposes, the general partner must be a corporate body resident in the Island.

Trusts

A Trust is not a "person" for income tax purposes and like a partnership is not a taxable entity in its own right. Income arising as the result of a trust will be assessable on the trustees or, if distributed, the beneficiaries. For the purposes of Manx income tax , the expression "Manx trust" includes -

(i) trusts made in the Isle of Man under Manx law that are managed and controlled in the Isle of Man ; and

(ii) foreign trusts that are managed and controlled in the Island.

This can give rise to a number of different taxation scenarios -

(a) a Manx trust in which -

(i) the beneficiaries reside in the Isle of Man; and

(ii) all the income of the trust is distributed each year,

the beneficiaries fall to be assessed to income tax on the income received;

(b) a Manx trust in which -

(i) one or more of the beneficiaries reside in the Isle of Man; and

(ii) a part or all of the income for any year is not distributed,

the trustees will be liable to tax on the part not distributed and the beneficiaries on the amount that has been distributed;

(c) a Manx trust in which -

(i) the beneficiaries do not reside in the Isle of Man; and

(ii) all the income of the trust arises outside the Island or from "approved" sources in the Island e.g. bank interest,

whether or not the income is distributed no liability to income tax will arise. This enables the income to be accumulated or distributed according to the needs of the trust.

Any Manx trust that gives rise to a liability to income tax in the Isle of Man , either directly on the trustees or indirectly on the beneficiaries, is required to lodge a copy of the trust deed with the Income Tax Division and submit an annual return of income and expenditure.

Chapter 5

Financial regulation, policies and structures

5.1 Policy

It is inherent in the Island's approach to the Financial Services Industry that the industry must be reputable and well-regulated. The high quality and good reputation of the Island's Financial Services Industry is considered to be essential for the Island's long term success in this field. To put it at its lowest, any instance of failure of regulation would be seen as counter-productive to the Island's external reputation and long-term interest and would be treated, within the Island, as a serious matter.

The Island's policy is, therefore, to regulate its finance industry to international standards and to regularly update its arrangements to keep abreast of developments. U.K. legislation and regimes of regulation are highly influential and, although there are significant differences as U.K. practice is adapted to suit the Island's requirements, the Island's arrangements are recognisably similar to those applying in the United Kingdom.

5.2 Development of Regulation

Regulating the Financial Services Industry is evolutionary in nature and the Island has constantly sought to improve its regulation in parallel with the growth in the Industry, also taking into account developing technology and law and practices elsewhere.

The first of the current generation of dedicated regulatory authorities was created in 1983 when the Financial Supervision Commission was formed following the collapse of the Savings and Investment Bank.

The activity of the Commission's early years focused on introducing Know Your Customer Guidance Notes, Anti-Money Laundering Guidelines, closing down smaller or potentially unstable banks, ensuring proper capital adequacy and ring fencing systems were in place. Following this initial housekeeping period, the Commission's attentions turned to regulating funds and fund managers through the introduction of the Financial Supervision Act 1988. The Act, which lays down structures and standards for Collective Investment Schemes and their managers, also introduced "gateways" enabling the Commission to communicate effectively with other international regulators, law enforcement bodies, the Isle of Man Treasury and other persons with whom it is essential for the Commission to have comprehensive communication arrangements.

These provisions were largely based on the newly introduced United Kingdom Financial Services Act "gateways" and ensured parity of communication and co-operation.

With banking and scheme business well ordered, the Commission turned its attentions to introducing the Investment Business Act in 1991 in order to ensure that those financial services businesses that were not able to rise to the standards newly required in the United Kingdom following the introduction of the Financial Services Act, were not attracted to the Isle of Man as a jurisdiction of lesser standard. From the earliest days, the Commission has conducted robust on-site compliance testing visits as well as the prudential style visit where broader management issues are discussed.

In 1993, the Investment Business Amendment Act 1993 was introduced. This significantly increased the Commission's investigation powers, and accordingly the Enforcement Division was established with the particular task of policing the perimeter, and taking strong action against those found in breach of the Banking, Investment or Collective Investment Schemes legislation.

The second of the new generation of regulatory authorities is the Insurance and Pensions Authority. It was originally established as the Insurance Authority in 1986 and became the Insurance and Pensions Authority in January, 1997, following the addition to its responsibilities of the role of developing a regulatory framework for pension business.

The Authority has successfully overseen the development of the diverse insurance industry on the Island.

A recent initiative will see the introduction of registration requirements for insurance intermediaries carrying on general business (as opposed to life and investment intermediaries already regulated by the Financial Supervision Commission). These general insurance intermediaries will be required to register with the Insurance and Pensions Authority under the Insurance Intermediaries (General Business) Act 1996 and to comply with certain criteria, including the requirement to have acceptable professional indemnity insurance. The market comprises some 20 independent intermediaries and a large number of tied agents.

The Pensions Bill, more wide-ranging than the United Kingdom equivalent, is to be introduced later this year, and will give the Insurance and Pensions Authority the legislative framework to regulate pension funds to the same high standard and effectiveness as insurance companies.

An Insolvency Bill is also included in the legislative programme for 1998/99. The policy of the Government is to achieve a sensible revision to its existing insolvency provisions, to take account of recent changes in the market place. There is no intention at this time to change extensively the liquidation system, more a fine tuning of the current provisions. A provision to allow corporate recovery procedures to be implemented will be included in the Bill as a new measure.

The Treasury and Tynwald have both given their support to a full-time office of Official Receiver being established. Provision for this will also be included in the Bill.

The next major development in relation to the regulation of financial services on the Island will relate to Corporate Service Providers.

As in the United Kingdom, there are currently, in the Isle of Man, no restrictions as to who can form and administer companies. However, in November, 1997, a consultative paper was issued by the Council of Ministers entitled "A Consultative Paper on the Licensing of Corporate Service Providers". The consultative paper proposed the licensing of all persons and/or bodies corporate who:

(a) form or sell companies by way of business;

(b) provide a registered office or accommodation address by way of business;

(c) provide directors (themselves or others) by way of business.

Further particulars on this initiative are shown in Section 12.

This is seen as the first of a series of developments to which the Council of Ministers has publicly committed itself and which will introduce additional regulation to the company and trust areas of business (see Section 17 below for the background to the Council of Ministers' report of April, 1992, which contained the public commitment).

In furtherance of this broad strategy, the Isle of Man Treasury established a Working Party in March, 1998, to examine the supervision of companies in the Isle of Man and to look at ways in which existing corporate law may be more effectively enforced. The Working Party has met a number of times since March and on 18th June, considered a report based on its preliminary findings. The findings were categorised into areas which related to company registry issues, company supervision issues, domestic and international solvency issues and a number of other points relating, for example, to measures to wind up in the public interest and provisions for disqualification of delinquent directors.

The principal finding of the Working Party was that there was a clear need to establish a Companies Supervision Commission and the Working Party has produced a report for submission to the Treasury and consideration by the Council of Ministers. It is anticipated that the development of such a Commission will go hand in hand with the introduction of the regulatory system for Corporate Service Providers and that both will progress in the near future.

This initiative can be shown to have wide political support. At the April 1998 sitting, Tynwald resolved:

> "That Tynwald is of the opinion that the legislation relating to companies should be reviewed to ensure that companies incorporated in the Island or incorporated elsewhere and registered under Part XI of the Companies Act 1931 are controlled and managed in compliance with principles and procedures which are consistent with the best interests of the Island's economy and its reputation."

The area of Trust regulation will be addressed subsequently as part of the broad strategy of reviewing and extending regulatory arrangements, in order of priority, to company service providers, companies and trusts.

The Isle of Man Government has established high standards with its legislation and practices in respect of the regulatory authorities established and responsibilities allocated since 1983. The same rigorous approach and pursuit of quality is driving the further regulatory initiatives which are in process or in prospect.

5.3 Agencies Involved in the Regulation and Supervision of the Financial Services Sector

There are a number of agencies of the Isle of Man Government who have roles to play in the regulation and supervision of the Financial Services Sector. Of these, the most important are the Financial Supervision Commission and the Insurance and Pensions Authority.

(a) The Financial Supervision Commission

The Financial Supervision Commission is an independent Statutory Board. It is directed by seven Commissioners, of whom six are all appointed from within the Island and are non-executive; these include a Chairman, who is a member of Treasury. The only Executive Commissioner is the Commission's Chief Executive.

Commissioners are appointed by Treasury subject to the approval of Tynwald. Commissioners may have other financial sector interests - for example, non executive directorships of licenceholders - but must declare their interests in advance of appointment and absent themselves from any Commission debate where there may be a conflict of interest.

Currently the Commissioners are all residents of the Isle of Man, selected for their professional experience of the Island as an international finance centre. Their expertise includes previous directorships of major banks and telecommunications organisations, a clearing bank's trust operation, a major private bank, and senior management experience of collective investment schemes, the building society industry, information technology for the financial services sector, mainstream clearing banking together with expertise in economics and financial services marketing. Additionally, the Commissioners are professionally qualified in areas of banking, economics, law and investment business management.

The Commissioners sit, formally, every two weeks. The Commission considers a wide range of issues, from policy matters to individual licensing decisions.

The Commission's costs are primarily met from fees paid by institutions and schemes which it licences and authorises. In 1998/99, the Commission's estimated costs are £1.56 million and its income £1.1 million.

The Commission has, since its inception in 1983, interpreted and published its remit as follows:

(a) The purpose of having a banking and financial centre is to provide measurable economic benefits to the Island;

(b) The Isle of Man has nothing to gain from permitting activities or institutions which provide shelter for or facilitate the activities of criminals, and

(c) Institutions established on the Isle of Man and their customers will benefit from standards of licensing and supervision which reflect best practice and are acceptable to supervisory authorities in other jurisdictions.

The main functions of the Commission include:

(i) the licensing and supervision of banking institutions under the Banking Acts of 1975 to 1998;

(ii) the licensing and supervision of investment businesses under the Investment Business Acts 1991-93;

(iii) the authorisation, recognition and regulation of collective investment schemes under the Financial Supervision Act 1988;

(iv) the authorisation and supervision of building societies under the Building Societies Act 1986; and

(v) various miscellaneous functions under the Companies Acts 1931-92

The staff of the Commission numbers 23, of whom 15 are professional regulators, 4 administration staff whose responsibility includes personnel and information systems, and 4 who provide secretarial services. The Commission encourages employees to develop their professional skills and qualifications and, accordingly, staff hold a variety of relevant qualifications including memberships of the Institute of Bankers, Insurance Institute, Securities Institute, the Institute of Chartered Secretaries and the Institute of Certified Accountants. Of the professional regulatory staff, 7 have international employment experience and all have international market experience gained through their regulatory activities, international training and mutual assistance visits.

The Commission is divided into four divisions:

(1) Supervision

Supervision delivers a "one stop shop" FSA style integrated regulatory operation, covering banks, building societies, investment and securities businesses, collective investment schemes and credit unions.

The Supervision Division is committed to the concept of approaching regulation in a manner that recognises the conglomerate nature of many of its licenceholders and therefore multi-skilled teams carry out the on-site compliance testing visits.

(2) *Administration*

Administration is responsible for financial controls, IT systems and Human Resources issues, as well as providing the Secretariat services for the Chief Executive's Office and the Commission itself.

(3) *Policy and Special Projects*

The role of Policy is Commission wide and is focused on ensuring the Commission's operational divisions continue to deliver "leading edge" supervision by evaluating international developments and following a programme of re-evaluation of existing policies and practices. Additionally, Policy and Special Projects carries out Disciplinary Actions against licence-holders where a compliance matter arising from Supervisory meetings takes a more serious turn.

The Commission's policy in respect of disciplinary action is robust. Work has resulted in:

(i) 5 notices under Section 10 of the Investment Business Act have been issued. This has resulted in 5 individuals being barred from the industry because their conduct has fallen below acceptable standards.

(ii) 2 petitions to court to wind up licenceholders in the public interest, plus

(iii) 1 voluntary cessation of a licenceholder's activity following an investigation.

These various procedures have full rights of appeal and, on each occasion, the Commission's decisions, or petition, has been upheld.

(4) *Enforcement*

The Enforcement division has, as its primary function, the responsibility of investigating and taking appropriate action against those who conduct investment, banking or scheme business without the appropriate authorisation.

Additionally, the Division has prophylactic and preventative roles which it delivers through, for example, collation of intelligence, identification of trends, active monitoring, close liaison with other international regulatory and law enforcement bodies and through seeking to educate the public by means of articles, lectures and conferences.

In terms of results, the Division's work has taken 45 matters to court, secured 45 victories, including 19 petitions to wind up in the public interest and 2 Restitution Orders. Over £11 million has been returned to investors from over 14 jurisdictions.

The work of the Division is unusual because, so far as the Commission is aware, no other offshore jurisdiction delivers an equivalent function.

The Commission attaches much importance to its international memberships - for example, the Commission is a member of the International Organisation of Securities Commissioners (IOSCO), the Enlarged Contact Group (ECG) on collective investment schemes, and of the Offshore Group of Banking Supervisors (OGBS) established by the Basle Committee on Banking Supervision.

The Financial Supervision Commission has entered into memorandums of understanding with the Investment Managers Regulatory Organisation, the Law Society of England and Wales, the Institute of Chartered Accountants for England and Wales, the Isle of Man Law Society, the U.K. Securities and Futures Authority, the Australian Securities Commission, the London Stock Exchange, the U.K. Securities and Investments Board, FIMBRA and LAUTRO. Other memoranda are under discussion.

The Commission publishes Guides which fully explain its licensing policy and includes as Appendices to each guide, all relevant codes of conduct applicable to each different type of licenceholder.

FINANCIAL SUPERVISION COMMISSION

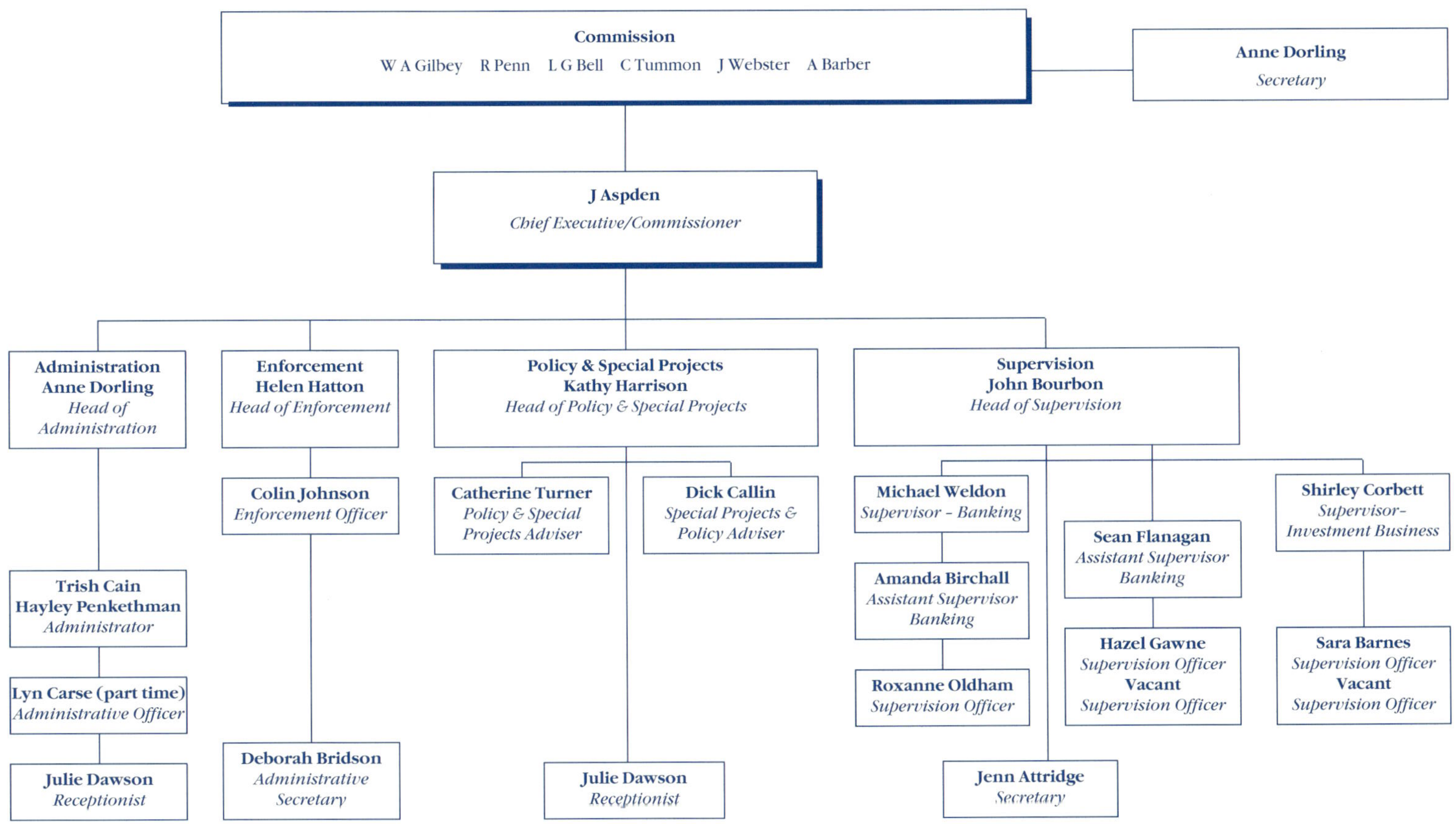

(b) The Insurance and Pensions Authority

The Insurance and Pensions Authority is a Statutory Board established under the Insurance Act 1986 and it has responsibility for the regulation and development of the insurance and pensions sector in the Isle of Man. Specifically, it is responsible for the authorisation and ongoing supervision of Isle of Man companies carrying on insurance business in or from the Isle of Man and for companies incorporated elsewhere which carry on insurance business on the Island. Following the introduction of the proposed pensions legislation, it will also have responsibility for regulating pension schemes and those persons who conduct and administer pensions business on the Island.

The Authority is directly responsible, within its statutory remit, for ensuring the administration of the Insurance Act 1986. The Authority, subject to the approval of the Treasury, sets and administers its own budget, appoints according to its own terms and conditions, its own staff and decides, without Government interference, how to best manage its affairs to ensure that its statutory role is fulfilled.

The Authority may be subjected to such change as Tynwald, reflecting democratic process, may consider appropriate.

The Members of the Insurance and Pensions Authority are appointed by the Treasury, subject to the approval of Tynwald. They comprise a chairman (who must be a Member of Tynwald) and at least two other persons. Currently, there are four members of the Insurance and Pensions Authority in addition to the Chairman. One of these is the Chief Executive of the Insurance and Pensions Authority. All the members have substantial experience of the international insurance industry, and include an actuary and an accountant. Two of the members are not resident on the Isle of Man and travel to it from the United Kingdom for the Insurance and Pensions Authority's regular meetings.

Members of the Authority may have other interests connected with the insurance sector on the Isle of Man, for example non-executive directorships, but must declare their interests in advance and take no part in any decisions of the Authority where there may be a conflict of interest.

The Insurance and Pensions Authority is a policy making body and it, therefore, delegates much of its responsibility on a day-to-day basis to the holder of the office known under the Insurance Act 1986 as the Insurance Supervisor. The Insurance Supervisor is also the chief executive officer of the Insurance and Pensions Authority.

The Authority meets, on average, every six to eight weeks.

The Isle of Man was the first jurisdiction to receive Accreditation under the United Kingdom's Financial Services Act (Section 130) as a Designated Territory. This acceptance by the United Kingdom of the quality of the Authority's regulatory framework allows the Island's insurers to sell in and through the United Kingdom.

The Island's insurance market place has a close and natural affinity with the United Kingdom and other international jurisdictions, particularly through ultimate beneficial ownership, shareholder, reinsurance, investment management and other links. Relationships with the relevant regulatory authorities are essential and these have been fostered over many years. In a United Kingdom context, typically, given the nature of the Authority's role and its designation, these bodies comprise:

(i) The Insurance Directorate of HM Treasury;

(ii) Formerly the PIA and the Building Societies Commission, but now the new regulator.

Meetings to discuss matters of regulatory concern and interest are a normal behaviour pattern.

The Insurance and Pensions Authority's role is regulatory. It is to administer the Insurance Act 1986. Within that, it has established the following prime objectives - its "Mission Statement":

"1. For the Authority:

To create, for the Insurance and Pensions Authority, a decision making and operational structure that is pragmatic and manageable; one in which it retains policy decision making but operates on the basis of delegated decision making to its Executive.

2. For the Regulatory Environment:

To provide a regulatory environment that is compatible with international standards

3. For the Administrative Environment:

To ensure an administration system that is technologically advanced and provides a cost effective support to the regulatory functions falling within the Insurance and Pensions Authority's remit."

The Insurance and Pensions Authority currently has an establishment of nine full-time staff. This comprises the Chief Executive and five other regulatory staff (one of whom is in the process of being recruited); a member of staff responsible for general business development, public relations activities and office services; and two administrative support staff. The Authority is committed to recruiting additional staff as they become necessary.

The Authority's establishment is supported by appropriate data processing systems which comprise, amongst other facilities, a relational data base and an analytical reporting mechanism for all businesses it authorises and supervises. The system is there to assist staff in the execution of the statutory mandate of the Authority. The system helps to highlight potential problems and therefore assists in the prioritisation of regulatory action that may be decided upon.

The Insurance and Pensions Authority's projected expenditure for the financial year 1998/99 is £718,800, of which some £565,000 will be recovered in licence fees.

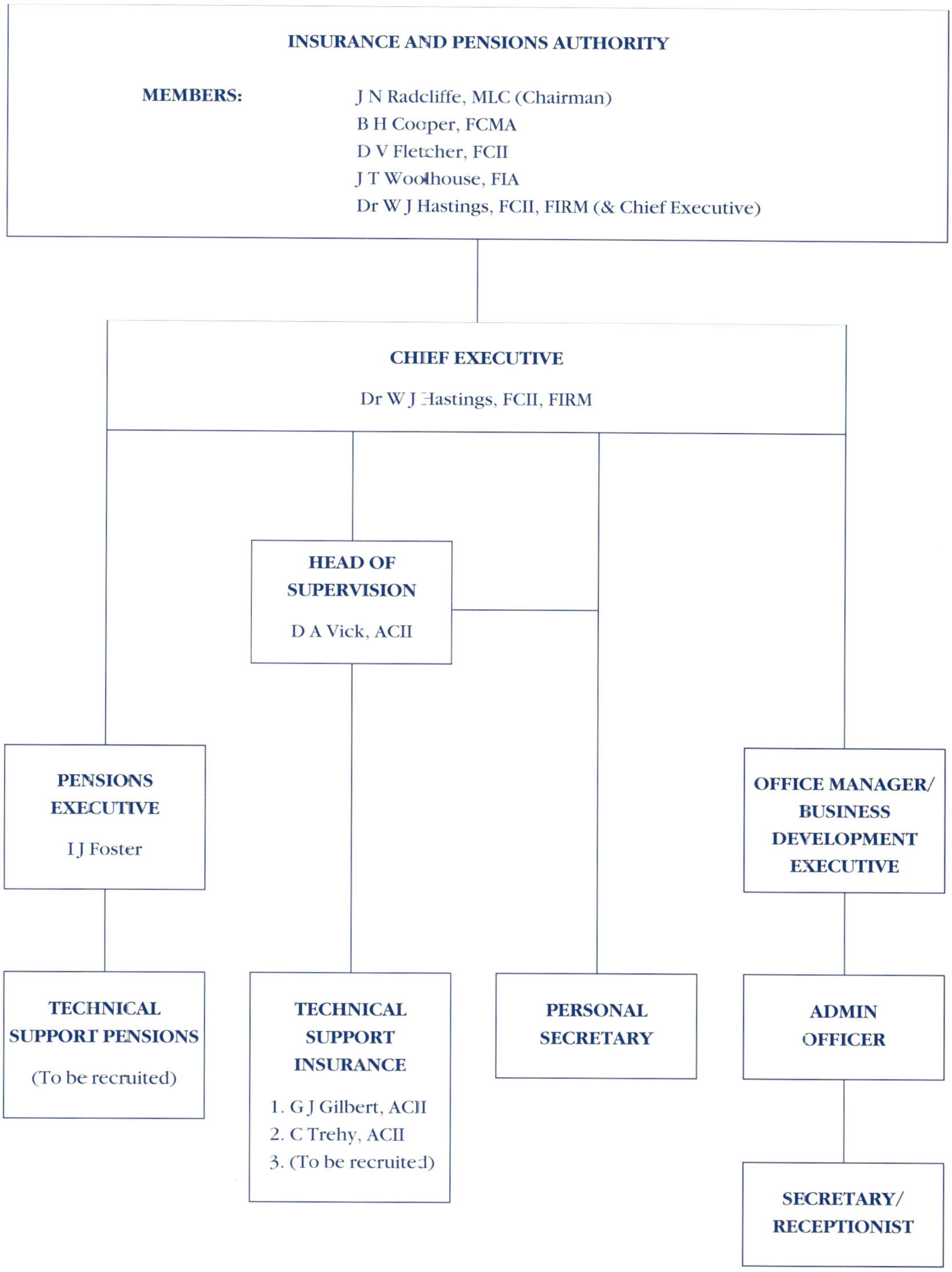
INSURANCE AND PENSIONS AUTHORITY
MEMBERS:
J N Radcliffe, MLC (Chairman)
B H Cooper, FCMA
D V Fletcher, FCII
J T Woolhouse, FIA
Dr W J Hastings, FCII, FIRM (& Chief Executive)
CHIEF EXECUTIVE
Dr W J Hastings, FCII, FIRM
HEAD OF SUPERVISION
D A Vick, ACII
PENSIONS EXECUTIVE
I J Foster
OFFICE MANAGER/ BUSINESS DEVELOPMENT EXECUTIVE
TECHNICAL SUPPORT PENSIONS
(To be recruited)
TECHNICAL SUPPORT INSURANCE
1. G J Gilbert, ACII
2. C Trehy, ACII
3. (To be recruited)
PERSONAL SECRETARY
ADMIN OFFICER
SECRETARY/ RECEPTIONIST

(c) Other Agencies

Although not regulators, the Attorney General's Chambers, the Police, the Companies Registry, Customs and Excise and the Income Tax Division have important roles to play in investigation and enforcement.

5.4 Regulatory Legislation and Supervision

This section reviews the regulation and supervision of the core financial services of banking, building societies, collective investment schemes, fund management, investment businesses, insurance and pensions.

(a) Financial Supervision Commission

The Financial Supervision Commission is responsible for regulating banks, building societies and investment businesses, collective investment schemes and fund managers that operate in or from the Isle of Man. It was established in 1983 with the remit:

> *"To take such steps as appear to it (FSC) to be necessary or expedient for the effective supervision of the private financial and commercial sector in the Island"*

In fulfilling its remit, the Commission has adopted the following Mission Statement:

> *"To promote and secure high standards of integrity, solvency and competence within the Manx financial services industry, in order to engender an environment in which financial institutions provide quality products and services for the economic benefit of the Island*
>
> *To fulfil its Mission, the Commission will:*

(a) set and publish standards designed to:

(i) protect investors' and depositors' interests;

(ii) promote the financial stability of financial institutions;

(iii) promote the highest standards of competence and professional qualifications;

(iv) protect the integrity of the financial community;

(v) protect the reputation of the Isle of Man.

(b) monitor compliance with the standards, taking prompt action where necessary.

(c) take steps to investigate and, where appropriate, prosecute those engaged in unlicensed investment or banking business.

(d) co-operate with other regulators and play a full part in the development of international regulatory standards.

(e) assist Government in reviewing the promoting legislation relevant to the Financial Services Industry.

(f) seek the participation and support of the industry in achieving its objective."

Effective regulation is ensured through publishing a clear licensing policy, focusing on sound initial licensing decisions - no amount of regulation can make up for a poor initial licensing decision - followed up by thorough compliance testing of adherence to codes of conduct and standards.

More detail about the Commission's approach to the regulation of particular parts of the financial services industry is given in Sections 6 and 7.

(b) Insurance and Pensions Authority

The basic regulatory framework for insurance business is set out in the Insurance Act 1986 (as amended)("the Act") and the more detailed requirements are included in regulations made under the Act. The Act states that any person carrying on insurance business in or from the Isle of Man (and in respect of an Isle of Man incorporated company, anywhere in the world) must be authorised to do so by the Insurance and Pensions Authority, unless exempted by the Act or the regulations. Many of the principles on which the system of supervision and its requirements are based are similar to those adopted in the United Kingdom and other major financial centres.

The Insurance and Pensions Authority considers that it is an important part of its role to examine, on an ongoing basis, the effectiveness of the legislation to ensure that the interests of the policyholders and of the Isle of Man are protected and enhanced. To this end, a number of changes have been made to the legislation since it was originally put in place (for example, the solvency margin requirement for life companies was increased and the amount of information required to be filed was also increased).

The work which is currently being undertaken in respect of pensions is another example of this role.

Not only are the requirements set out in primary and secondary legislation but also in a set of Guidance Notes. It is therein that policy is clarified, for example, what the Authority considers to constitute "Management" in the Island; what its view is on the matter of discretionary trusts; what, for the purposes of an application must comprise the constituent documents.

Most activity associated with the regulation and administration is conducted off-site. All documentation, Authority meetings and formal regulatory meetings are normally held within the Authority's offices although supervisory meetings may be held at the offices of the company, particularly in respect of life assurance companies.

The Authority uses external professional advisers as and when necessary. Typically, these would be lawyers, accountants, actuaries, systems specialists, insurance and pension specialists. In all instances, these are seen as complementary. Additionally, in an enforcement context, law enforcement agencies will be utilised.

In particular, all life insurer returns, in addition to being reviewed internally, are referred to a United Kingdom firm of consulting actuaries, Watson Wyatt, for actuarial review. Watsons report, certainly annually, on a case by case basis, and sometimes more frequently depending on circumstances. No life insurer is authorised without actuarial review of the business proposals made.

The Insurance and Pensions Authority is a member of the International Association of Insurance Supervisors and is also an active founding member of the Cross-Border Group of Insurance Supervisors, thereby bringing its weight to progressing regulatory standards around the world.

More detail about the Authority's approach to regulation is given in Section 8.

5.5 Investor Protection

Protection of investors and depositors, both on and off the Island, is at the heart of the Government's regulatory policy. The Government is very aware that the majority of the Island's customers do not live on the Island itself and therefore their interests may not most immediately be represented through the normal Parliamentary/constituency system. However, it is to the credit of the Island's regulatory system that investor and depositor protection for non-Manx resident customers, as much as for residents, is enshrined in legislation and in the Island's regulatory policy. These protections are derived from 3 main areas:

1. Firstly, as described under 5.4, through the strong initial licensing test, and by keeping "greenfield site" and low competence operations out of the jurisdiction.

2. Once licensed, the investor/depositor protection is further enhanced by active compliance testing, ensuring solvency is properly monitored and compliance with, for example, Client Money rules.

3. If, despite all measures under 1 or 2, a bank, building society or scheme collapses, the Isle of Man offers statutory "safety net" protection via:

(a) Banks/Building Societies

The Depositors Compensation Scheme (Banking Business [Compensation of Depositors] Regulations 1991) offers 75% of the eligible protected deposit liability up to a maximum of £15,000 to any one depositor. Whilst the Isle of Man scheme is similar to the United Kingdom provisions, Island depositors are additionally protected, above United Kingdom provision, in one respect, namely that the Isle of Man Scheme extends to all currencies whereas the United Kingdom scheme is applicable only to Sterling deposits. The Depositors Compensation Scheme is a fund to which contributions are levied from licenceholders if required.

(b) Collective Investment Schemes

For those investors who place their monies in Authorised Schemes, protection, in the event of disaster, can be taken from the Authorised Collective Investment Schemes (Compensation) Regulations of 1988. These provide for a fund, financed by contributions from the regulated institutions.

Similarly, this protection has United Kingdom parity and was successfully evaluated by HM Treasury in its examination of the Isle of Man regulatory regime prior to gaining Designated Territory Status and was again evaluated as satisfactory in a recent follow up review.

It is thought that the Isle of Man is the only offshore jurisdiction to offer a Depositors Compensation Scheme as well as a dedicated enforcement team.

(c) Insurance Companies

The Isle of Man has a statutory policyholders compensation scheme for life assurance companies. The scheme was introduced in 1988 (initially as a voluntary arrangement pending appropriate legislation) and is now constituted under the Life Assurance (Compensation of Policyholders) Regulations 1991.

It is designed to provide benefits for policyholders of up to 90% of the actuarially-assessed liabilities of any life company which becomes unable to meet its obligations. Unlike a number of other schemes in other jurisdictions, there is no upper monetary limit on the amount of compensation which can be paid to an individual protected policyholder.

In the event of it being activated, the scheme would be financed by a levy on the remaining life assurance companies which are part of it, up to a maximum of 2% of the actuarial liabilities. The Insurance and Pensions Authority is the designated scheme manager.

Since the scheme was introduced, it has not been called into operation.

Chapter 6

Banking

business

6.1 Policy

The activities of banks and deposit-takers are closely supervised and controlled in the Isle of Man. The Isle of Man Government and the Financial Supervision Commission are well aware of the political, economic and social damage which can occur as the result of a bank failure. Furthermore, because of the possibility of damage spreading through a reduction of confidence, banking supervision should aim to be a seamless robe. It is this principle which underlies the International Concordat on banking supervision drawn up by the Basle Supervisors' Committee, to which the Isle of Man is a subscriber. This provides for the sharing of responsibilities between supervisory authorities.

The licensing policy for banks and deposit taking institutions is based on an evaluation of quality encompassing a wide variety of criteria, not least of which is culture. The policy is not based solely on a world ranking system, though it does take account of IBCA ratings and other similar information.

The Commission does not license privately owned banks, nor any licenceholders whose ownership rests ultimately in a discretionary Trust. All licenceholders are subject to a stringent initial and ongoing "fit and proper" test which encompasses examining institutional and senior management's competence, integrity and solvency.

The Commission's licensing policy does not permit "greenfield site" or start up operations. All applicants have to satisfy the Commission that they have a satisfactory track record in acceptable jurisdictions. Additionally, the licensing policy does not admit licenceholders unless the Commission can be satisfied that the parent company operates in a jurisdiction which is in compliance with the recommendations of the Basle Committee on Banking Supervisors and that the Commission can establish satisfactory inter-regulatory relationships with the home regulatory authority.

The Isle of Man is not party to the EU "passporting" arrangements and therefore makes individual decisions on each licensing application received.

6.2 Coverage

In the Isle of Man, banking business is defined in section 1 (1) of the Banking Act 1998 as being " .... *a business which includes the carrying on of any one of the following activities:*

(a) the receipt of deposits;

(b) the payment and collection of cheques."

This is a deliberately wide definition which may encompass persons whose business may technically fall within the definition but who clearly are not intended to be caught by the definition. The Commission, therefore, has power under section 1 (3) of the Banking Act 1998 to declare in writing that the business is not to be treated, for the purposes of the Act, as banking business.

Conversely there is power, again under section 1 (3) of the Act, for the Commission to declare that a business is to be treated as banking business and on the making of such a declaration the Act shall apply accordingly to that person's business. This power might be used, for example, to ensure proper supervision of the holding companies of banks licensed in other jurisdictions.

Under section 1 (4) of the Act, the Treasury may by order modify the definition of banking business in section 1 (1) of the Act.

Additionally, there is the definition of banking business under section 2 (2) of the Banking Act. This sub-section provides that a person shall be treated as carrying on a banking business:

"(a) *in the Island if that person carries on a banking business outside the Island and establishes a representative office in the Island; or*

(b) from the Island if that person -

(i) is a company incorporated in the Island under the Companies Acts 1931 to 1993; or

(ii) is a body corporate incorporated outside the Island which is registered under part XI of the Companies Act 1931,

and carries on or holds itself out as carrying on a banking business outside the Island, whether on its own behalf or on behalf of any other person in or outside the Island."

In sub-section 2 (a), " representative office" means any office which in any way appertains to any banking business carried on by a person, other than an office from which that person actually carries on that business.

These provisions encompass all Isle of Man incorporated companies, whether resident or non-resident, and all foreign companies having a place of business on the Island which carry on banking business in or from the Island or abroad.

The establishment on the Isle of Man of holding companies for banks licensed in other jurisdictions will also require a licence under the Banking Act and the activity of managing in the Isle of Man banks licensed in other jurisdictions is dealt with by Section 3 of the Banking Act.

The Commission may issue two types of banking licence: a Domestic Banking Licence or an Offshore Banking Licence.

6.3 Domestic licences

There are two categories of Domestic Banking Licence :-

(i) Unrestricted

A domestic banking licence permits a bank to conduct a full range of banking business with customers both in the Isle of Man and elsewhere. The licenceholder must have a real presence on the Isle of Man This means that it must satisfy the Commission that it has on the Isle of Man its own management and staff, discrete and secure premises, and adequate systems and resources to conduct banking business.

(ii) Restricted

A domestic banking licence may be issued - subject to certain restrictions placed on the licenceholder.

6.4 Offshore licences

Offshore Banking Licence ("Managed Bank")

This type of licence allows a bank (the managed bank) to engage an appropriately licensed bank (an Approved Manager) in the Isle of Man - to manage the Isle of Man banking operations on behalf of the managed bank. This is achieved by way of the establishment of a branch in the Isle of Man or by way of a locally incorporated subsidiary - which is "managed" by an "Approved Manager". This is an option chosen by a bank wishing to establish an offshore presence without incurring the cost of establishing a full banking operation on the Island. Such managed banks may not conduct business with local residents, but the mechanism allows the development of the offshore presence into a full operation over a period of time. It is, in effect, an opportunity for the managed bank to 'put a toe in the water'.

From a regulatory point of view, this system also has attractions in that the Commission would have a strong existing relationship with the approved manager and will have already satisfied itself of the manager's control procedures and fit and proper status. Clearly, the managed bank must also satisfy the Commission's initial and ongoing licensing requirements and the system does not provide a facility for a managed bank to be licensed at any sort of lower standard.

There are also two categories of Offshore Banking Licence:

(i) Unrestricted Licence

— permits retail banking business from off Island clients (as agreed with the Commission)

— permits interbank business - on or off island

(ii) Restricted Licence

— excludes retail business whether on or off Island

— permits intra-group banking business - as agreed by the Commission

The disclosure - to the Commission - of beneficial ownership of a licenceholder is required and once a licence is issued, changes in ownership control require the Commission's prior consent. The Commission treats a change of ownership control, though not necessarily a change in the structure of ownership, as equivalent to a new licence application. The Commission must be aware, at all times, of the identity of the owners of an institution licensed under the Banking Act.

6.5 Licensing and supervision

The centrepiece of the Commission's licensing policy is the "fit and proper" test. This test seeks to ensure that licenceholders have in the past done and will continue in the future to do what is correct and fair in relation to the banking business for which they are licensed or are seeking a licence.

It is impossible to define conclusively the interpretation of the term "fit and proper". However, the Commission considers that three broad criteria should be applied:

(i) integrity

(ii) solvency

(iii) competence

Essential aspects of the Commission's regulatory arrangements concern banks and financial resources and cover against risk. As regards financial resources, the Commission operates policies in relation to:

— capital adequacy and

— liquidity

For capital adequacy, the Commission requires that all institutions meet a minimum risk asset ratio of at least 10%. The requirements, however, also have regard to qualitative and business factors and many institutions have minimum ratios set well above 10%. In addition, there is a "trigger" ratio set slightly above the minimum, to provide an early threshold for consultation with the Commission and prevent a breach of the minimum. In line with Basle principles, the risk asset ratio has assumed much greater importance over the gearing ratio, as a supervisory tool. A minimum for the latter would normally be set at between 50:1 to 80:1 according to the size of capital.

Quarterly returns of maturing assets and liabilities by time band and different currency, provide the focus for supervising liquidity. Each institution is expected to have in place a statement of liquidity policy, which must be agreed as appropriate for its business with the Commission. Compliance is monitored against this policy.

There are, in addition, full requirements regarding accounts, auditing, record keeping and management information.

While the Commission seeks to ensure that the owners of banks are suitable and fit and proper and recognise their obligations to depositors, the responsibility for the prudent and successful conduct of the bank's business rests with the directors and management. The Commission, therefore, imposes certain regulatory requirements upon the directors and management of licensed banks.

These include:

- *Dual Control ("Four eyes control")*
- *Board Supervision and Control*
- *Local Directors and Company Secretary*

Supervisory information is required from banks at the end of each calendar quarter. (Offshore banks are required to report every six months). This information includes:

(i) an analysis of assets and liabilities;

(ii) an analysis of core and supplementary capital, current period's profit and loss account, provisions, large exposures, related party transactions and certain memorandum items; and

(iii) a maturity analysis, together with a geographical analysis of the non-bank deposit base and a coded listing of the banking institution's ten largest depositors.

Large exposures less than 10% of the capital base incur no special supervisory requirements. Those of 10% but less than 25% of capital have to be reported separately each quarter, with full details of the borrower, purpose of loan, security, etc. Exposures of 25% or more of capital require the prior consent of the Commission and will only be allowed if covered by a guarantee or loan take-over agreement provided by the parent.

In addition, a rolling programme of on site compliance visits is carried out by a team of Supervision Officers. Meetings may take the form of prudential visits, or blitz focus visits, the aim of which is a short but detailed examination of one small area of operation:-

for example, account opening procedures.

6.6 Combatting abuses

The Commission has long been aware of the risk of abuse of the Island's banking facilities by criminals. As long ago as 1985, the Commission introduced a "Know Your Customer" policy, designed to alert the banks to the dangers of doing business with people they did not know and of relying solely upon introductions from the marketplace. The Know Your Customer policy requires licenceholders to seek evidence of identity, to enquire as to the nature of the business and activity of the customer and to monitor the activity of any doubtful accounts.

Since then, the Basle Supervisors Committee has introduced its Statement of Principles in December, 1988; the G7 countries formed a Financial Action Task Force on money laundering in June, 1989, which produced its Recommendations in April, 1990; and in December, 1990, the Joint Money Laundering Working Group in the United Kingdom produced its Guidance Notes for Banks and Building Societies. The Commission has produced Guidance Notes based on those issued by the Joint Money Laundering Working Group and has updated them regularly; in 1998 the Isle of Man enacted all crimes money laundering legislation which is fully compliant with the current EU Directive.

6.7 Legislation

The Banking Act 1998 provides substantial powers for supervisory, disciplinary and enforcement purposes. The Act enables the Commission to:

— inspect the books, accounts and transactions of a licenceholder

— search premises, seize documents using such force as necessary

— require persons to attend and answer questions

- issue public statements
- require persons to produce documents
- remove a licence
- restrict a licence
- attach conditions upon a licence
- issue directions
- declare an individual to be no longer fit or proper
- petition the Court to appoint a Receiver
- petition the Court to make a Restriction Order
- petition the Court to fine or convict in regard to a range of offences

Additionally, and unusually in the respect of an "offshore" centre, the Act provides facility to the Commission to use these powers against those who, on reasonable grounds, are suspected of conducting banking business without a licence.

All these powers are used regularly and robustly by the Commission in the execution of its functions.

In respect of offences and penalties, the Commission, is, as already explained, a prosecuting authority in its own right. The Banking Act 1998 contains criminal penalties in several significant areas.

Chapter 7

Investment

and Securities Business

7.1 Investment Businesses

There are a number of different categories of licence issued by the Financial Supervision Commission under the Investment Business Acts 1991-93, although all are subject to the Commission's stringent fit and proper test licensing principles.

Category 1

Group A - persons who do not control clients' money or assets and who arrange deals only in a restricted range of investments (i.e. unit trusts, life and pensions products). Such persons may provide investment advice (other than to occupational pension schemes and collective investment schemes) on other types of investments, but may not arrange deals in them, except for subscriptions to new share issues.

Group B - tied agents selling the products of only one product company. Such person may control clients' money provided that the product company which the agent represents has provided an indemnity in respect of clients' monies to the Commission in an acceptable form.

All Category 1 licenceholders require minimum net tangible assets of £5000 and further details of this are available in the various Codes of Conduct.

There are 30 Category 1 licences issued.

Category 2

Group A - persons who arrange deals in any investment instrument but who do not receive or control clients' money; or persons who arrange deals in a restricted range of products (as in Category 1) but who may control clients' money; or persons who act as share distributor or provide share registration or accounting services to collective investment schemes established in approved jurisdictions; or persons who act as investment adviser to occupational pension schemes and/or collective investment schemes.

Group B - managers of collective investment schemes, but only where the manager is administered by a licenceholder who is authorised as Category 4 business.

Category 2 Group A licenceholders must have minimum net tangible assets of £5000 and 3 months' annual audited expenditure to be maintained as liquid capital whereas Group B requires minimum net tangible assets of £5000 and one month's annual audited expenditure to be maintained as liquid capital.

Category 3

Investment managers and dealers who control clients' money and assets, managers of restricted collective investment schemes (except as provided in Category 2 above), including managers of more than one 'exempt restricted scheme' within the meaning of Section 11 (7) of the FSA 1998; or persons acting as investment manager to collective investment schemes established and operated in other jurisdictions; or managers of authorised collective investment schemes; or investment businesses, other than those included in Categories 1, 2 and 4.

Category 3 licenceholders require minimum net tangible assets of £25000 and 3 months' annual audited expenditure to be maintained as liquid capital.

Category 4

Licenceholders providing administrative services to managers of authorised and/or restricted collective investment schemes (except as provided for in Categories 2 and 3 above).
Category 4 licenceholders require minimum net tangible assets of £100,000 and 3 months' annual audited expenditure to be maintained as liquid capital.

Category 5

Category 5 licences relate to those acting as stockbrokers. There are 7 licences issued to stockbrokers on the Isle of Man, 4 being the London Securities and Futures Authority members and 3 non-SFA members. Those members of the SFA are required to adhere to the Financial Resources requirements of the SFA. Those which are not are required to have minimum financial resources of £50,000 for an agency broker and £100,000 for a broadscope firm, together with a liquid capital requirement of 3 months' annual audited expenditure.

In order to be licensable, investment activity must be carried on **by way of business**. Thus, as in the United Kingdom, private transactions are excluded from the scope of the Investment Business Act 1991. Investment activity is licensable if it is carried on **in** or **from** the Island. Also, in practice, the Commission is unlikely to grant a licence to an organisation unless it is managed and controlled in the Island, as to do so would leave the Island vulnerable to unscrupulous operators with no accountability in the Isle of Man. This provision extends the scope of the Financial Supervision Commission's provisions further than equivalent sections of the United Kingdom Financial Services Act.

An offence is committed not only if a person conducts investment business without a licence, but also if he conducts activity with a licence but in contravention of any conditions of that licence. The conditions which are attached to investment business licences concentrate, in most circumstances, upon the scope of activity which a licenceholder is permitted to conduct.

When an investment business licence is issued, a series of Regulatory Codes apply to that licenceholder. Should a licenceholder breach any of the Regulatory Codes, the Commission is empowered to take regulatory action.

The range of activities which are included in the definition of "investment business " is wide and a variety of differing disciplines and requirements are involved. The Commission, therefore, adapts its regulatory and supervisory approach accordingly, but the basis of the Commission's licensing policy is not affected.

As with Banking licence applications already described (Section 6), the basic test applied by the Commission to any licence application is designed to seek to ensure that licenceholders (whether individuals or firms) have in the past done and will continue in the future to do, what is correct and fair in relation to the investment business for which they are licensed or are seeking a licence.

It is important to note that the fit and proper test is both an initial test at the time of granting a licence and a continuing test in relation to the conduct of the business and the relationship with the Commission.

The Commission issues Investment Business Licenses subject to conditions. A breach of a licence condition imposed is both a criminal offence and can lay a licenceholder open to action for damages at the suit of any private investor who suffers loss.

In general, as noted above, licence conditions are normally restricted to defining the scope of business which may be conducted by the licenceholder, but they may be augmented at any time by the imposition of "special" licence conditions, designed to respond to particular problems.

Because, whatever the category of licence, a person conducting business in contravention of licence conditions risks criminal prosecution and/or civil action at the suit of anyone who suffers loss, the Commission has sought to place the weight of its regulatory ability upon the observance by licenceholders of Regulatory Codes.

These Codes, which are intended to set standards of good practice and behaviour, apply to each licenceholder. Should a licenceholder breach any of the Regulatory Codes, the Commission is empowered to take regulatory action. This action will be graded, dependent upon the seriousness of the breach.

The Regulatory Codes cover the following:

- **Financial Resources and Reporting**. These requirements are directly related to the scope of Investment Business conducted by the licenceholder. In addition, all Investment Businesses are required to maintain an adequate amount of professional indemnity insurance cover which is defined in published guidelines but is a minimum of £100,000. Licenceholders are required to submit periodical financial statements to the Commission.

- **Clients' Money**. This Code requires clients' money to be held in segregated and properly designated accounts with an approved bank on trust for investors. The Code also aims to ensure that clients' monies are properly recorded, reconciled and controlled.

- **Clients' Investments**. The principal objective of this Code is to ensure that adequate arrangements are maintained to ensure that clients' title documents are kept safely, are properly recorded, identified, segregated and controlled. A licenceholder can place clients' title documents only with eligible custodians and such title documents should be reconciled at least half yearly.

- **Conduct of Business**. This Code describes the general principles and standards of conduct which the Commission expects licenceholders to adopt in their dealings with clients and others.

- **Audit Requirements**. Auditors of Investment Businesses (other than those businesses which do not control clients' money or assets) are restricted to those firms of appropriate experience which are covered by professional indemnity insurance of not less than £10 million. The Code requires the auditor to make specific reports to the Commission in relation to the Regulatory Codes.

- **General Requirements**. This Code lays down several fundamental requirements, perhaps the most important of which is that the business of licenceholders who handle clients' money must be conducted on a day to day basis by at least two individuals (known as the "four-eyes" principle).

- **Advertising**. The Advertising Code lays down general principles relating to advertisements to which licenceholders must adhere.

The Commission's staff seek to visit each licenceholder at least once a year at a pre-arranged time when the licenceholder is required to demonstrate that the requirements of the Regulatory Codes have been met. It is likely that the Commission's staff will wish to see evidence that record keeping requirements have been complied with, that client agreements have been signed, etc. Where appropriate, the Commission also conducts unannounced focus visits, the objects of which are to call unexpectedly and examine one small area of operation - for example, Handling Clients Money - to check procedures and standards within the licenceholder.

7.2 Collective Investment Schemes

The Financial Supervision Commission is charged with the responsibility for administering the provisions of the Financial Supervision Act 1988 (FSA 1988) as they relate to collective investment schemes. The Act, which came into operation on the 1st November, 1988, provides for the regulation of three classes of collective investment scheme:

1. Schemes **authorised** by the Commission under Section 3 of the FSA 1988;
2. **Restricted** schemes within the meaning of Section 11 of the FSA 1988; and
3. Schemes **recognised** by the Commission under Sections 12 and 13 of the FSA 1988

Authorised Schemes

Currently, only authorised securities schemes (of which Government and other public securities funds are a particular type), money market funds, umbrella funds, funds of funds and feeder funds are eligible for authorisation under section 3 of the FSA 1988.

To obtain an Order under section 3 of the FSA 1988 declaring a scheme to be an authorised scheme, the proposed manager and the trustee must apply to the Commission in accordance with section 2 of the Act.

The provisions of section 3 of the Act include a requirement that both the proposed manager and trustee of the scheme must be "authorised persons", i.e. "a person holding a licence granted under section 3 of the Investment Business Act 1991 or such other classes of permitted persons (within the meaning of that Act) as may be prescribed".

So far as proposed managers are concerned, they must hold an investment business licence and only banking institutions licensed under section 6 of the Banking Act 1998 are eligible to act as trustees of authorised schemes.

An application for authorisation must be accompanied by a certificate signed by an Advocate to the effect that the contents of the scheme's constitutional documents comply with the requirements of the Financial Supervision (Authorised Collective Investment Schemes) Regulations 1988. Once a scheme has been granted authorisation, any **proposed** alteration to the scheme, or any proposal to replace either the manager or trustee, must be notified **in writing** to the Commission.

Authorised schemes must be constituted either as:

(a) unit trust schemes whose trust deed is made under and governed by the law of the Isle of Man; or

(b) open-ended investment companies to which Part 1 of the Isle of Man Companies Act 1986 applies.

Therefore, a scheme constituted under the law of another country or territory, or which is not constituted in the Isle of Man as either a unit trust or open-ended investment company, is not eligible for authorisation.

Authorised schemes are able to be promoted to the general public in the Isle of Man. In addition, because the United Kingdom Government has granted the Isle of Man "designated territory status" for the purposes of Section 87 of the United Kingdom Financial Services Act 1986, an Isle of Man authorised scheme, which is of a category specified in the Schedule to the United Kingdom Designation Order may give notice to the Securities and Investment Board ("the SIB") in the United Kingdom for recognition of the scheme pursuant to Section 87 of the United Kingdom Financial Services Act 1986. Upon receiving recognition, a scheme may, subject to certain requirements, be promoted to the general public in the United Kingdom.

Reciprocal arrangements operate between the Isle of Man, Jersey, Guernsey and Ireland in respect of authorised schemes and Isle of Man authorised schemes are also subject to "fast track" approval procedures in Hong Kong and Australia. In addition, the Japanese Securities Dealers' Association have agreed that Isle of Man authorised schemes, which have been recognised by the Securities and Investments Board in the United Kingdom, are eligible for promotion to Japanese residents.

Restricted Schemes

The Commission has not prescribed what types of Restricted schemes may be established as this would be contrary to its policy of providing a flexible regulatory framework in which operators can innovate and develop new products to meet the changing and developing needs of the market place. However, the Commission will have views as to the acceptability or desirability of certain types of schemes and may, in such circumstances, refuse to grant or extend a manager's licence to enable it to manage a scheme of that particular type. Generally, the Commission does not favour the establishment of restricted schemes whose primary investment objective is to invest in:

(a) assets which cannot be readily liquidated or accurately valued through a recognised investment exchange or market; or

(b) assets which are outside the normal scope of exchange traded instruments and where the Commission may have difficulty in assessing a licenceholder's ability to manage those assets.

Therefore, schemes investing in real estate, certain precious metals and gemstones, would not normally be acceptable.

Restricted schemes are not subject to any direct approval or authorisation process. However, the manager is required to give the Commission written notice, in accordance with section 11 (2) and (3) of the FSA 1988, within fourteen days of the scheme becoming or ceasing to be a restricted scheme, and so the Commission is able to exercise some control over the establishment of restricted schemes in the Isle of Man through its licensing of restricted scheme managers.

The Commission's approach to the regulation of restricted schemes differs significantly from the regulation of authorised schemes. For restricted schemes, the Commission has sought to avoid comprehensive prescriptive regulation, leaving managers free to innovate and develop new products, whilst at the same time upholding investor protection by requiring strict disclosure of all material matters to potential investors.

Restricted schemes are subject to a general prohibition on promotion in the Isle of Man but they may be promoted to the public outside of the Isle of Man. Any advertising of a restricted scheme carried out by a licensed manager outside the Isle of Man must be in compliance with the requirements of the Advertising and Scheme Particulars Regulations and the Financial Supervision Commission (Advertising) Regulatory Code.

Certain restricted schemes are not subject to the provisions of Section 11 of the FSA 1988, or the regulations made thereunder. Section 11 (7) provides that, subject to the provisions of subsections (8) to (10), a scheme is exempted from Section 11 if:

(a) it has less than 50 participants; and

(b) the relevant constitutional document prohibits the making of an invitation in any part of the world to the public or any section of it to subscribe for or purchase units in the scheme.

In line with the intention of Tynwald when the legislation was passed, the Commission has regarded "exempt" restricted schemes as private arrangements, and therefore not subject to regulation.

The Professional Investor Fund was introduced in December, 1995, and is a special sub-category of the Isle of Man's restricted collective investment schemes classification. The launch of the PIF introduces a regulatory approach which provides a framework for the design of mutual fund vehicles which are suitable for sophisticated and high net worth individuals and market professionals. Such investors require a different level of regulation to that which applies to ordinary investors. The PIF regime provides this and brings with it flexibility and the potential for cost savings.

The Professional Investor Fund in itself is not subject to approval or regulation by the Commission. However, the operator of a PIF (whether a fund manager, third party fund administrator or bank) must obtain the Commission's prior approval before operating PIFs.

The PIF regime is based around the Financial Supervision (Professional Investor Fund)(Exemption) Order 1995 which defines the conditions for a PIF. Certain other secondary measures contribute to the regulatory approach for PIFs.

Recognised Schemes

The term "recognised scheme" refers to schemes which originate from outside the Isle of Man and which, subject to recognition being granted by the Commission, may be promoted to the general public in the Isle of Man.

Recognised Schemes are able to be promoted to the general public in the Isle of Man. However, anyone wishing to promote recognised schemes in the Isle of Man must either hold an investment business licence or be exempt from requiring such a licence and the scheme itself must comply with the notification requirements of the Commission and must maintain specified facilities on the Isle of Man for the service of investors.

As already mentioned, all recognised schemes must comply with the requirements of the Financial Supervision (Scheme Particulars) Regulations 1988, as they apply to authorised schemes. However, recognised schemes from designated countries or territories may be exempt from complying with some or all of the requirements of Schedule 1 to the Scheme Particulars Regulations.

Ongoing regulation of Collective Investment Schemes takes the form of formal and informal relationships between the various parties connected to the Scheme, Manager, Custodian, Trustee and Commission.

Active compliance visits are carried out on all Fund Managers following much the same format as described under both Banking and Investment Business headings.

From time to time, the Commission has had to intervene and has powers under the Investment Business Act and the Financial Supervision Act to take a broad range of actions including public notices, searches, enquiring, directions, appointment of inspectors, winding up in the public interest, etc.

Powers of inspection and investigation mirror those already described under the Banking Act 1998 and include powers to:

- Inspect the books, accounts and transactions of licenceholders
- Search premises and seize documents using such force as necessary
- Require persons to attend and answer questions
- Issue public statements including naming institutions, or persons, and warnings to the public as appropriate
- Require persons to produce documents
- Remove a licence

- Issue directions
- Declare an individual to be no longer fit and proper
- Petition the Court to make a Restriction Order
- Petition the Court for the appointment of a receiver
- Petition the Court to fine or convict in regard to a range of offences - see above.

Similarly to the Banking Act, the IBA provides, unusually, for these powers to be used in respect of those who, on reasonable grounds, are suspected of conducting investment business without the appropriate licence.

CHAPTER 8

INSURANCE AND PENSIONS BUSINESS

8.1 Insurance Business

Principal Regulatory Requirements and Powers

The principal ongoing regulatory requirements and powers of the Insurance and Pensions Authority under the Act and Regulations include the requirement:

(i) that all companies maintain a minimum solvency margin requirement at all times (the solvency margin being the amount by which the company's assets exceed its liabilities). The level of the required solvency margin will vary depending on the type and volume of business written;

(ii) to restrict, for solvency purposes, the admissibility of certain categories of assets;

(iii) to require an authorised insurer to maintain assets in a particular form or in a particular place;

(iv) to separate from those of shareholders the assets of the policyholders which are held in the Long Term Business Fund;

(v) for life assurance companies applying for authorisation, to appoint an actuary who satisfies the criteria laid down by the Insurance and Pensions Authority (ie. he is a Fellow of the Institute or Faculty of Actuaries or equivalent and has relevant experience). The appointed actuary will be responsible for certifying annually that the company's liabilities to its policyholders do not exceed its assets and that the financing of the company is adequate;

(vi) to make quarterly returns for at least three years of operation (these may then be waived if the Supervisor gives consent); and

(vii) to submit audited annual accounts and supplementary information (for life companies this includes an actuarial report and valuation by the appointed actuary). The annual returns must be certified by the directors;

(viii) to impose conditions on an existing authorisation or to revoke it;

(ix) to require an authorised insurer to supply information to it from time to time or on a particular matter;

(x) to investigate the transactions and inspect the books and records of an insurer and to seize them if necessary. This power extends to companies suspected on reasonable grounds of carrying on business without authorisation;

(xi) to petition the Court for the winding up of an insurer if it is unable to pay its debts or has failed to satisfy any obligation to which it was subject under the Act;

(xii) to petition for the winding up of a company if it has carried on insurance business without being authorised;

(xiii) in the event of a change in ownership, control or management, to be notified (The Authority has the right to object to the new principals);

These and other provisions are strictly enforced and action is taken when appropriate, including the imposition of special conditions and petitioning the Court to wind up. The Act contains special provisions in respect of the winding up of companies carrying on life assurance business. In this latter respect, most liquidations have been voluntary liquidations of solvent companies, reflecting merger and acquisition activity.

Under section 24 of the Insurance Act 1986 and section 10 of the Insurance Intermediaries (General Business) Act 1996, the Insurance and Pensions Authority may disclose formally to other agencies information which it has obtained. These agencies include the Financial Supervision Commission and other authorities which appear to the Insurance Supervisor to exercise in a country or territory outside the Isle of Man functions corresponding to those of the Insurance and Pensions Authority. Information may also be disclosed with a view to the institution of, or otherwise for the purposes of, any criminal proceedings, whether under the Insurance Act 1986 or the Insurance Intermediaries (General Business) Act 1996 or otherwise.

Principal Matters Relating to Authorisation

Before authorising any company to carry on insurance business in or from the Isle of Man, the Insurance and Pensions Authority must be satisfied as to:

(i) the fitness and propriety of the proposed shareholders and ultimate beneficial owners, directors and managers;

(ii) the financial resources of the proposed company. This includes consideration of a detailed three-year business plan and will include an assessment of the ability of the shareholders to commit further resources should that be necessary; and

(iii) the type and volume of business to be underwritten and the exposures to be accepted.

With regard to paragraph (i) above, extensive checks are carried out before any decision to authorise is taken. These checks will include reference to agencies on the Isle of Man and internationally.

Other matters on which the Insurance and Pensions Authority must be satisfied before authorisation is granted include:

(i) that the company has actually been incorporated;

(ii) that the beneficial interests in shareholdings have been disclosed;

(iii) that the agreed amount of capital has been paid up (the amount of capital required will vary depending on the type of business to be underwritten);

(iv) that the quality and suitability of the company's reinsurance programme;

(v) that the company will operate as a bona fide insurance company, underwriting and accepting or declining insurable risks and that it is not to be used merely as a vehicle to collect risk-free income and commissions;

(vi) that the proposed auditors have the required amount of professional indemnity insurance, this being a minimum of £10 million;

(vii) that proper books and records will be maintained on the Isle of Man at all times.

Initially, all companies have to maintain a deposit in a licensed bank in the Isle of Man and must submit a business plan to the Insurance and Pensions Authority.

All companies must be managed and controlled on the Isle of Man and maintain their books and records on the Island at all times. (This is an important aspect of the Insurance and Pensions Authority's control over the companies which it supervises - lead action has been taken within the last year in conjunction with insurance regulators in the United Kingdom, Ireland and Guernsey to enforce this provision in respect of one particular company). The Authority must be satisfied that the proposed management arrangements are adequate and appropriate for the business to be underwritten.

Principal Matters Relating to Ongoing Supervision

The Insurance and Pensions Authority attaches considerable importance to the value of maintaining contact with the insurance companies which it regulates in order to remain aware of their business philosophies and objectives. It combines this with detailed examinations of information submitted to it regularly by every company, as set out below:

(i) Quarterly returns containing specified information for at least the first three years of operation (these may then be waived if the Supervisor gives consent); and

(ii) Audited annual accounts and detailed supplementary information. For life companies, this includes an actuarial report on the valuation of liabilities by the appointed actuary. The annual returns must be certified by the directors.

The quarterly returns allow the Insurance and Pensions Authority to compare actual performance against the business plan. They also allow it to see at an early stage any significant developments and problems within the business, to discuss these with the company and, if appropriate, take action.

The annual returns, signed off as "true and fair", form the basis of the detailed annual review of the business. The accounts have to be prepared in accordance with standard formats. In addition to the accounts themselves, all companies have to submit supplementary information.

On-site inspection is not routinely currently part of the supervisory regime. Where inspections are undertaken, they relate to specific enquiries.

General Companies

For all general companies (including captive insurance companies), this supplementary information includes analyses of the individual classes of business underwritten and the development of claims, in total and for individual years. It also includes information about the company's reinsurance programme and has to set out details of material changes being made to the company's business. From this information the company's current financial position can be assessed and also an assessment made of its likely future position. As noted above, any material changes to the business must be advised and, particularly during the early years of operation, must be incorporated in a revised business plan. This must be submitted to the Authority and may result in additional capital being required or other changes to the management structure being made.

Life Companies

For life companies, the supplementary information includes a more detailed analysis of the company's business than is possible in the accounts themselves. As mentioned above, the actuarial report on the valuation of liabilities prepared by the appointed actuary must also be submitted with the returns. For companies in their early years of operation, a revised three year business plan must be submitted. The business plan forms a very important part of the examination of the company's position - differences between actual and planned experience may highlight potential problems within a company (for example, differences between planned and actual expenses are analysed to identify the reasons for any discrepancy).

The actuarial report for life companies includes details of the assumptions made by the appointed actuary in making his valuation of the liabilities. It will include an analysis of any additional and contingency reserves which he considers it appropriate to include in the total amount of liabilities.

Following receipt and examination of the returns, any matters of concern are discussed with senior management of the company. For life companies, the examination includes a review of the returns by the Insurance and Pensions Authority's appointed consulting actuaries. The consulting actuaries provide technical advice to the Insurance and Pensions Authority on both specific cases and matters of general interest or concern.

8.2 Pensions Business

The Principles of the Proposed Regulatory Framework

In order to create a prudent regulatory framework for domestic and international pensions, the Isle of Man has used the United Kingdom Pensions Act 1995 as one of its prime models. However, in certain regards, the Isle of Man has, after taking extensive advice from pension professionals, other regulators and the not insubstantial input from the Authority's consulting actuaries, deviated from the legislative requirements in the United Kingdom.

Unlike OPRA in the United Kingdom, the Isle of Man Government Insurance and Pensions Authority will require all trustees to apply for authorisation. This will involve stringent "fit and proper" requirements. The Authority believes that the quality of the trustees is paramount in the prudent management of pension schemes.

The whistleblowing requirement in the United Kingdom compels the actuary and the auditor to whistleblow to OPRA. The Isle of Man proposals compel all parties involved in pension scheme management to whistleblow. These parties will include the actuary, the administrator, the auditor, the investment manager and the trustees.

All pension schemes will be required to submit scheme accounts to the Insurance and Pensions Authority for assessment. Accounts must be submitted no later than 6 months following the end of the scheme year. In the United Kingdom, it is the scheme membership who must be provided with a copy of audited accounts no later than 7 months following the end of the scheme year.

All scheme governing documentation will require to be submitted to the Insurance and Pensions Authority for authorisation.

All schemes will require to have their scheme documentation certified by an Advocate (solicitor) to confirm that all documentation conforms to the legislation.

The Isle of Man framework will apply to personal pensions as well as occupational schemes, domestic and international.

A funding requirement, to be known as the Technical Funding Requirement ("TFR"), will be introduced. The objective will be to ensure that the funding position remains appropriate to the current and future liabilities of the scheme.

The Income Tax Division is in consultation with the Inland Revenue over the proposed changes to ensure they conform to the existing reciprocal arrangement relating to the transfer of pensions between the United Kingdom and the Isle of Man.

Chapter 9

Regulation of companies and directors

Types of Company	31 March 97	31 March 98
Resident	20,030	20,431
Non-resident	10,200	10,648
Tax exempt		
• general	10,729	13,080
• insurance companies	183	183
International Companies	28	39
Limited Liability Companies (LLC)	30	95
International LLC	5	20
Total	**41,205**	**44,496**

9.1 Types of Company

There are a variety of different company types and structures identifiable within the Island and company formation and administration represents a significant part of the Island's financial services business. As is indicated in section 5.2 above and 17 below, there is an intention to introduce additional controls and regulation into the areas of companies and also trust business and proposals in this regard are and have been the subject of formulation and consultation.

The type and variety of corporate structure has evolved in response to commercial demands and the various forms of companies in evidence are identifiable in other competing jurisdictions. The Government's approach to company development and regulation has been to recognise the company as a valid form of business vehicle, to encourage the development of legitimate company business and to operate a registration system in relation to companies that is based on equivalent U.K. legislation. Companies engaged in specialist financial areas such as banking, insurance and investments, are, in addition, subject to regulation by either the Financial Supervision Commission or the Insurance and Pensions Authority, whichever is appropriate.

This strategy has not been sufficient to enable the Island to avoid isolated incidents where companies registered in the Island have been involved in activities which have attracted adverse public comment. It is, primarily, in an attempt to remedy this situation that the Island is proposing additional regulatory measures.

The main body of Isle of Man company law is set out in the Companies Acts 1931 to 1993, the 1931 Companies Act being the principal Act. The eight amending Companies Acts were enacted in 1960, 1961, 1968, 1974, 1982, 1986, 1992 and 1993 and are construed as one with the principal Act. The principal Act is also supported by a number of Orders, Rules and Regulations that have been made in exercise of the powers conferred by the Acts and certain other Acts of Tynwald, for example, the Fees and Duties Acts 1989.

Many of the provisions of Manx company law are derived from comparable United Kingdom provisions, and are recognisable as such.

There are 3 main classes of company registration provided for in the Island's legislation:

(a) those registered in the Isle of Man under the Companies Acts 1931-1993;

(b) those incorporated elsewhere and carrying on business within the Isle of Man under Part XI of the principal Act;

(c) those registered in the Isle of Man under the Limited Liability Companies Act 1996.

9.2 Responsible Agencies

The Companies Registry is responsible for registering companies; maintaining the public record of all registered companies; requiring compliance with statutory obligations, when necessary; charging statutory fees, and striking off defunct companies.

The Companies Registry is part of the Registries Division which, in turn, is the largest of the five divisions which make up the General Registry. Its responsibilities are broadly comparable to those of the Registrar of Companies in the United Kingdom. It does not form a part of the Financial Supervision Commission.

The responsibilities of the Companies Registry in relation to corporate entities are to:

(a) approve of the proposed company/ business name;

(b) verify the completeness and accuracy of registration documents;

(c) issue certificates of incorporation/ registration;

(d) oblige corporate entities to maintain their public record in the Companies Registry as required by legislation;

(e) charge and collect statutory fees and duties;

(f) remove the names of corporate entities from the register if they fail to comply with their statutory obligations. The consequence of this is that the company ceases to be able to trade legally;

(g) refer to the Attorney General's Chambers any prosecutable transgression discovered or brought to the Registry's attention;

(h) confer with the Financial Supervision Commission and other Government agencies wherever it is appropriate to fulfil its statutory obligations.

These responsibilities are carried out with 20.5 (f.t.e.) staff.

The Financial Supervision Commission has licensing, regulating and enforcement responsibilities in respect of companies conducting financial business.

The Insurance and Pensions Authority is responsible for authorising, regulating and enforcement responsibilities in respect of companies conducting Insurance and Pensions business.

9.3 Isle of Man Registered Companies

The liability of Isle of Man companies may be:

- limited by shares - where the liability of its members is limited to the amount, if any, that is unpaid on the shares held by them.

- limited by guarantee, with a share capital - where the liability of its members is limited to such amount as the members may respectively undertake to contribute to the company in the event of it being wound up.

- limited by guarantee, without a share capital - where the liability of its members is limited to such amount as the members may respectively undertake to contribute to the company in the event of it being wound up.

- unlimited, being a company which does not place any limit on the liability of its members.

An Isle of Man Company does not exist in law if it is not registered in the Isle of Man Companies Registry.

Companies in the Isle of Man are either registered under the Isle of Man Companies Acts and are Isle of Man companies, or they are foreign companies carrying on business on the Island and are registered under Part XI of the Companies Act. There is no corporate legal definition of residence or non-residence; these are definitions for corporate taxation purposes. Thus, an Isle of Man Company which is colloquially described as a "Non resident company" is a Manx registered company which has filed a declaration under S.2 of the Non-Resident Company Duty Act 1986. By so doing, it renders itself liable to pay Non-Resident Company Duty. Apart from the filing of the declaration under S.2 of the 1986 Act and paying Non-Resident Company Duty, such a company is no different to any other Manx registered company in the way that it may conducts its business. A non-resident company will, however, ensure that its business is controlled and managed outside of the Isle of Man so that it is non-resident for Manx income tax purposes.

At the present time, there is no requirement for an Isle of Man company to have a local agent. However, a foreign company which establishes a place of business in the Island and registers under Part XI of the Companies Act must deliver to the Registrar the names and addresses of one or more persons resident in the Island who are authorised to accept service of process of Court documents, etc., on behalf of the company.

Provided the name by which an Isle of Man Company intends to be known is not, in the opinion of the Registrar of Companies, undesirable, and the completed statutory registration documents are presented with the relevant fees, there is no power for registration to be refused.

A company is private when, by its Articles of Association, it prohibits any invitation to the public to subscribe for any of its shares or debentures, and it includes in its Memorandum of Association a provision that the company is private. Otherwise, it is a public company.

The statutory obligations on registration for public and private companies require the submission of the following documentation:

The Memorandum of Association

The Articles of Association

Form 1 - Particulars of First Directors and Secretary and Registered Office

with the correct fee.

Statutory obligations thereafter for public and private companies are to file details of certain changes, for example:

- the return in respect of each allotment of shares,
- the return in respect of a change of registered office,
- the return in respect of any change of directors or secretary,
- the return in respect of any charge created by a company,
- the annual return to be filed each year

There is no requirement to register the beneficial owner of a company.

The annual return must include details of the company's registered office, share capital, members, directors, company secretary and indebtedness in respect of registered charges. It confirms that the company is still in existence and it enables the public and the Chief Registrar to identify any changes during the proceeding year.

The contents of the files held by the Chief Registrar in his capacity as Registrar of Companies are available for inspection by members of the public upon payment of the appropriate fee.

A company is able to borrow against its assets. If however, the borrowing is secured by a charge of the type which is set out in s.79 of the Companies Act 1931, the company must register the charge with the Registrar of Companies in order to secure the priority of the charge against other creditors or a liquidator.

A public company is required to file a copy of its financial accounts with its annual return. Private companies are not required to file a copy of their financial accounts unless they are subsidiaries of Manx Public companies, or are liable to file accounts under the Timeshare Act 1996. They are, however, required to prepare and keep audited accounts to safeguard the 'interests' of their Members.

A company may not issue any form of application for its shares unless the form is issued with a prospectus which complies with the Companies Act and is registered in the Companies Registry.

Late filing of change details results in a penalty fee being charged. Failure to file an annual return prompts a letter of enquiry which, if not responded to within 2 months, results in a sequence of statutory written and public warnings which end in the defaulting company being struck off.

In the case of insolvency, the Companies Act provides for companies to be wound up:

(a) by the Court; or

(b) voluntarily (creditors' or members'); or

(c) subject to the supervision of the Court.

The principal method of dealing with an insolvent company is for a creditor or other interested party to apply to the High Court for the making of a winding up order. There are a number of grounds on which such an application can be made to the court, the usual ground being that the company is unable to pay its debts.

The Isle of Man does not have a full time Official Receiver but the High Court does appoint official receivers on an *ad hoc* basis.

In a winding up by the court, a liquidator of a company is appointed by the court and has full power to gather in and deal with the assets of the company. In winding up the affairs of a company, payments to creditors must be approved by the court. When the winding up is complete, the court formally orders the dissolution of the company and discharges the liquidator.

The Bankruptcy Act 1988 provides that the High Court of the Isle of Man shall assist courts having bankruptcy jurisdiction in "any relevant country or territory" which means the United Kingdom or any part thereof and any country or territory designated as such by an order made by the Council of Ministers.

	Public Companies	Private Companies
Registration Requirements	Name	Name
	Registered Office Address	Registered Office Address
	Memorandum and Articles of Association	Memorandum and Articles of Association
	Directors - Name, Home Address, Nationality & Occupation	Directors - Name, Home Address, Nationality & Occupation
	Secretary - Name, Home Address, Occupation	Secretary - Name, Home Address, Occupation
	Initial Subscribers	Initial Subscribers
	Capital Details	Capital Details
On-Going Requirements Requiring Notification/ Approval	Change of Name	Change of Name
	Change of Address	Change of Address
	Change in Capital	Change in Capital
	Change of Director/Secretary	Change of Director/Secretary
	Company Charges	Company Charges
	Prospectus for Share Issues	
	Annual Return and List of Shareholders	Annual Return and List of Shareholders
	Audited Accounts and Director's Report	
	Principal Activity	Principal Activity
	Resolutions	Resolutions

9.4 Non-resident Company Duty Act 1986

A company incorporated in the Isle of Man:

- the central management and control of which actually is located outside the Island; and
- which has delivered a non-resident declaration in the prescribed form to the Registrar of Companies,

is regarded as being non-resident for income tax purposes, at least until such time as:

- the company delivers a rescission of its non-resident declaration in the prescribed form to the Registrar of Companies; or
- the Assessor concludes that the central management and control of the company has, in fact, become based in the Island.

9.5 Foreign Incorporated Companies

These companies, if they establish a local place of business, are required, as opposed to being permitted, to register at the Companies Registry under Part XI of the Companies Act.

On registration, such companies are required to lodge:

- certified copy of the Charter, Statutes or Memorandum and Articles of the company, or other instrument constituting or defining the constitution of the company;
- list of directors and Secretary;
- name and address of one or more persons resident in the Isle of Man and authorised to accept on behalf of the company service of process and any notices required to be served on the company.

There is no requirement to declare beneficial ownership.

Statutory obligations thereafter are to notify the Companies Registry if any alteration is made to:

- the Charter, Statutes or Memorandum and Articles of the company, or other instrument constituting or defining the constitution of the company;
- directors (and Secretary);
- the name and address of agent.

A late filing fee is payable for the filing of any document outside such time limit as is prescribed in the Acts. Also, the Registrar is able to strike defunct Part XI companies off the register if he believes they no longer have a place of business in the Isle of Man and if they fail to respond to two written warnings and one public notice.

There are statutory powers to order general investigations into the affairs of or the winding up of a company registered under Part XI.

9.6 Limited Liability Companies (LLCs)

The features of LLCs, constituted under the Limited Liability Companies Act 1996, are:

(a) the company has a legal personality and capacity for the exercise of its purposes and powers;

(b) the members of the company will have their liability limited to the capital which they introduce;

(c) management rests with the members although a manager can be appointed;

(d) taxation of the Company will be similar to that of a partnership in that the profits can be divided amongst the members and taxed accordingly;

(e) it will have a life limited to a period not exceeding 30 years.

This form of company is used primarily for the holding of assets and is based on a model from the United States of America.

The regulatory regimes for LLCs are:

1. The Chief Registrar may strike the company off the register if the registered office has been abandoned or the annual return is not submitted. An LLC can also be wound up under Part X (Winding Up of Unregistered Companies) of the 1931 Companies Act.

2. The Treasury or a member of the company can apply to the Court to appoint one or more competent inspectors to investigate the affairs of the company and report as the Court directs.

9.7 Locally Administered Companies Registered Elsewhere

All companies incorporated outside the Isle of Man that establish a place of business within the Isle of Man are required to register under Part XI of the 1931 Companies Act and a consultative exercise is well advanced about the Licensing of Corporate Service Providers (See Section 12) in which consideration is being given to the further regulation of companies generally (See Section 5.2).

9.8 Directors

A company incorporated in the Island is required to have at least two directors who must be individual persons. Subject to the provisions of the Companies Acts, and the Memorandum and Articles, and to any directions given by special resolution, the business of the company shall be managed by the directors who may exercise all the powers of the company. The concept of a nominee director has no foundation in Isle of Man law.

If authorised by the company's Articles, the directors may, by power of attorney, appoint any person to be an agent of the company for the purposes of discharging the powers and duties of the company on such conditions as they may determine, including authority for the agent to delegate all or any of his powers.

If a Director grants a general power of attorney purporting to delegate his powers to a third party for an indefinite period of time, this may well be in breach of that director's fiduciary duty to the company.

Section 26 of the Companies Act 1992 provides that, where it appears to the Court that a person's conduct makes him unfit;

(a) to be a director or secretary of a company; or

(b) to be a liquidator of a company; or

(c) to be a receiver or manager of a company's property; or

(d) in any way, whether directly or indirectly, to be concerned or take part in the promotion, formation or management of a company;

the Court may make a disqualification order.

The Court may treat a person as unfit, where that body corporate or person:

(a) has been convicted of an offence on the Island or elsewhere which involves dishonesty;

(b) has been convicted on the Island or elsewhere in the last 25 years of any combination of 3 or more offences under the Isle of Man Companies Acts 1931-1993 or legislation having equivalent effect in any country or territory outside the Island;

(c) has been convicted of any offence under the Prevention of Fraud (Investment) Act 1968, the Banking Acts 1975-1998, the Insurance Act 1986, the Companies Securities (Insider Dealing) Act 1987, the Financial Supervision Act 1988, the Investment Business Acts 1991-1993 or legislation having equivalent effect in any country or territory outside the Island; or

(d) has failed to comply with an Order of the Court to rectify a default in relation to any provision of the Companies Acts.

These provisions are expressly stated to be "without prejudice to the generality" of the general test of unfitness.

There are a number of other "disqualification" provisions contained within the Companies Acts:

(a) Section 208, Companies Act 1931 which provides that where an Order has been made for the winding up of a company by the Court and the Official Receiver has made a report stating that, in his opinion, fraud has been committed by a person in the promotion or formation of the company or by any director or officer of the company in relation to the company since its formation, the Court may order that the person, director or officer concerned shall not, without the leave of the Court, be a director of, or in any way directly or indirectly be concerned in or take part in the management of a company for such period not exceeding 5 years as may be specified in the order;

(b) Section 259 (4), Companies Act 1931, which provides that where a person has been declared to be personally responsible for the debts or liabilities of the company on the grounds of "fraudulent trading" or has been convicted of "fraudulent trading", the Court may make a disqualification order for a period not exceeding five years.

Although there have been no instances of disqualification relating to these powers, the Financial Supervision Commission have used similar powers which enable them to declare persons unfit and improper on a number of occasions. These provisions are included within the Investment Business Acts 1991-1993.

Chapter 10

Partnerships

10.1 Policy

The partnership is, on the Island, as elsewhere, an acceptable form of business organisation. Legislation has been in place governing partnerships since 1909. As a form of organisation, it continues to be favoured by the professions, particularly lawyers and accountants.

For Manx tax purposes, partnerships are not assessed to income tax. It is the partners of the partnership who are assessed. The taxation treatment is, therefore, dependent upon where the business of the partnership is carried on and where the partners are resident for tax purposes.

Apart from the traditional unlimited partnership, the limited partnership has become a recognised form of organisation in Manx law.

10.2 Limited Partnerships

Limited partnerships are used for a number of purposes, for example, as investment vehicles for ship financing purposes. They are similar to the German KG (Kommanditgesellschaft) in that they have a general partner and a number of limited partners who are investors.

In a limited partnership, there are one or more general partners who are jointly and severally liable for the debts and liabilities of the partnership, and one or more limited partners who are liable for the debts and liabilities of the partnership up to the limit of their respective contributions to capital. A general partner may be a corporate entity. Limited partners contribute capital to the business, but are excluded from management of the partnership business. There are 51 limited partnerships registered, primarily involved with shipping and related services and investment holding business.

Limited partnerships are attractive because:

1. As a legal entity they are recognised and used throughout Europe and the rest of the world;
2. The limited partners' liability for the debts of the firm can be limited to their contribution of capital to the partnership.

Every limited partnership is required to maintain a place of business in the Isle of Man and have one or more persons resident in the Isle of Man authorised to accept service of any process or documents served on the partnership.

Registration of a limited partnership occurs when the partners send a statement to the Registrar detailing the firm name (the name in which the business is carried on), the general nature of the business, the principal place of business, the full name of each partner, the term, if any, for which the partnership is entered into, and the date of commencement, a statement that the partnership is limited and a description of every limited partner. The partners can also enter into agreements that govern the relationship between them, for example, the proportions in which profits and losses are shared.

The Registrar must be informed of any change in the principal place of business, character of the business, name and address of person appointed to accept service for the partnership, the liability of any partner if it becomes limited rather than general.

All limited partnership files are available for public examination in the Companies Registry and copies can be obtained of the contents on payment of the appropriate fee.

Chapter 11

Regulation of trusts and trustees

11.1 Trusts

Trusts have been recognised in the statute law of the Isle of Man for many years and the trust concept is now well established in the Isle of Man. The principles of trust law and equity as developed in England apply in the Island insofar as they are not contrary to any local rule or custom.

The general body of trust law in the Isle of Man is based on legislation and case law. That law has created a system which imposes duties on trustees of trusts governed by Manx law which, in general, is no less onerous than those imposed by the general system of trust law in England.

The various types and categories of trusts which are established under English law are also found in Manx law. Trusts are utilised for many and various purposes and play a useful role in commercial and private client situations in precisely the same way as they are used in the United Kingdom and elsewhere.

The advantages which trusts established in the Isle of Man may offer depend to a large extent on the legislation of other countries. In those cases in which the settlor and the beneficiaries are resident outside of the Isle of Man, the Assessor of Income Tax in the Isle of Man looks through the trust and no assessment to Manx income tax is raised in respect of it. It is often the case that professional advisers will submit a copy of the trust instrument to the Assessor together with confirmation that the settlor and the beneficiaries reside outside of the Isle of Man with a view to obtaining confirmation from the Assessor that no assessment to Isle of Man tax will be raised. Other than this, there is no obligation to declare the identity of the settlor and/or the beneficiaries of a trust to any person in the Isle of Man.

The principal legislation in the Isle of Man relating to trusts is set out in the Annex.

Most of the legislation is based on English law, save that under the Purpose Trusts Act 1996, trusts may be established to fulfil a particular non-charitable purpose rather than for the benefit of a particular beneficiary, which would not be possible in English law.

It should be noted that the Island's Fraudulent Assignments Act 1736 is analogous to the old Statute of Elizabeth in England and makes voidable any trusts set up with a view to defeating creditors whether or not such creditors were ascertained at the date of the creation of the trust. It is generally accepted, therefore, that so called "asset protection trusts" would be liable to be set aside under Manx law.

11.2 Trust Regulation

There is no formal requirement to register trusts although, as noted above, there is a well developed practice whereby trusts may be inspected by the Assessor of Tax, at the option of professional advisers.

There is, at present, no formal regulatory regime as such which applies to trusts, although it is the intention that persons who provide the services of professional trustees will be brought into the corporate service provider legislative regime in due course; all persons acting as professional trustees will have to show that they are fit and proper to act. The absence of a formal regulatory system for trustees and trusts in the Isle of Man means that, as in the United Kingdom, there are no reliable data about trusts managed on or from the Isle of Man.

It is important to note that, if trusts are utilised in relation to investment and/or pension schemes, then those trusts and the trustees thereof will be subject to regulation by the Financial Supervision Commission and/or the Insurance and Pensions Authority.

The Courts in the Isle of Man are able to enforce against trustees all the remedies which are available to plaintiffs in Chancery proceedings in the English Courts and in some important respects, such as in developing the duties of a protector (Steele v Paz Limited), the use of Norwich Pharmacal Orders to ascertain beneficial ownership of trust assets, and exploring the feasibility of remedial constructive trusts (Cotter v Cusack), the jurisdiction relating to trusts continues to develop in the Isle of Man and takes account of decisions in England and other jurisdictions.

Trusts established for charitable purposes may be enforced at the suit of the Attorney General on behalf of the public of the Isle of Man.

The Island's law in relation to trusts and the regulation of trust service providers is to be the subject of review.

Chapter 12

Regulation of corporate, trust and investment service providers

12.1 Corporate Service Providers

The Council of Ministers has asked the Financial Supervision Commission to devise a regulatory system for those who form and administer companies by way of business in, on or from the Isle of Man. Such businesses will be known as Corporate Service Providers (CSPs). A consultative document containing the Commission's proposals was issued in October, 1997, and final amendments to the proposed legislation are now being made.

The main provisions of the proposed system are:

that all persons (including bodies corporate) on the Isle of Man who:

— form or sell companies by way of business;

— provide a registered office or accommodation address for companies (whether Manx or otherwise) by way of business;

— provide directors (either themselves or through an associate) for companies by way of business;

will be required to be licensed. These persons will be known as Corporate Service Providers (CSP). It is intended that the list of licensable activities should be able to be amended by order.

CSPs will be required to be licensed by an appropriate Regulatory Body ("the Regulator"). The Regulator will license an applicant only if he can be satisfied that it is a fit and proper person (embodying the concepts of integrity, solvency and competence).

The Regulator may revoke the licence of a CSP if he believes that the CSP is no longer fit and proper.

The proposed legislation would also prohibit the incorporation of a Manx company by someone who is not resident in the Isle of Man. Furthermore, non-resident companies, exempt companies and international business companies will only be able to be incorporated by a CSP.

The main responsibilities of the CSP would include to "Know his Customer" and, where directors are provided, to take reasonable steps to ensure that those directors are suitable for their role, that they understand their duties, responsibilities and liabilities as directors.

A licensed CSP will be required to:

— adhere to a Code of Conduct;

— maintain sufficient working capital to enable it to meet its liabilities as they fall due;

— submit an annual return to the Regulator confirming compliance with the Regulator's requirements;

— submit ad hoc notifications to the Regulator, for example, when there are changes in management, ownership, etc., of the CSP or when any legal action is taken against the CSP.

The enforcement powers and rights of intervention envisaged are:

— Power to impose conditions/issue formal directions

— Power to issue public statements

— Power to require information

— Power to carry out investigations

— Suspension or withdrawal of licence

— Powers of restitution

— Fines

— Power to apply to the Court for injunctions.

Any information obtained by the Regulator when exercising his functions under the new legislation would be subject to legitimate confidentiality provisions.

It is intended to keep this legislation, as far as possible, a matter for civil law. It is, therefore, proposed that only the following should constitute a criminal offence:

— Acting as a CSP without being properly licensed;

— Knowingly or recklessly making false or misleading statements or providing false or misleading information to the Regulator; and

— Obstructing the Regulator during its carrying out of a statutory investigation.

The Regulation of Corporate Service Providers Bill is programmed to be introduced into the legislature during the next legislative session of Tynwald and, subject to Tynwald approval, is likely to become law in 1999. It is recognised that there will be significant resource implications required consequent upon the implementation of this legislation.

12.2 Lawyers

The Isle of Man Law Society was formed by the Law Society Act 1859 passed by Tynwald under which the Society was incorporated as a body corporate with perpetual succession. At the time, there were 29 practising Advocates in the Isle of Man.

In 1966, there were only 25 practising Advocates in the Isle of Man, which number reflected the then depressed state of the Isle of Man economy. By 1985, the number of practising Advocates had only increased to 33. In 1998, there are 89 practising Advocates and the Manx Bar has the necessary expertise to meet the requirements of the international finance community.

In 1986, Tynwald enacted the Legal Practitioners Registration Act 1986. This Act enabled legally qualified persons from outside the Isle of Man to come to the Isle of Man to work and provide legal services in most matters. There are 77 legal practitioners, other than Manx advocates, registered on the Island, most of whom are British barristers or solicitors.

Also in 1986, Tynwald passed legislation to introduce the Advocates Disciplinary Tribunal. This Tribunal consists of a legally qualified chairman appointed by the Governor, two persons nominated by the Board of Consumer Affairs (one of Government's Statutory Boards) and two persons nominated by the Council of the Law Society. All formal complaints against Advocates have, since 1986, been dealt with by the Advocates Disciplinary Tribunal. Prior to 1986, complaints were dealt with by the Law Society.

Advocates firms on the Isle of Man range from sole practitioners who primarily provide general advice, to larger practices with specialist departments providing advice and assistance in areas such as banking, insurance, aviation, shipping, trust, litigation and generally those legal services required of it by the finance sector. Many Advocates firms also employ specialist solicitors qualified in other jurisdictions.

Members of the Society who undertake Investment Business are required to apply to the Council of the Law Society for authority to do so as they are regulated by the Society in their conduct of such business. Practice Rules have been issued to the members in conjunction with the Financial Supervision Commission.

12.3 Accountants

The 1996 Census indicated that there were 444 qualified accountants on the Island.

All the major accountancy bodies are represented on the Island. The majority of accountants in the Isle of Man are members of the Institute of Chartered Accountants in England and Wales, the Association of Chartered Certified Accountants and the Chartered Institute of Management Accountants.

All Chartered Accountants on the Island are members of one of the three "British Isles" Chartered Accounting Bodies, ie. the Institute of Chartered Accountants in England and Wales, the Institute of Chartered Accountants in Scotland and the Institute of Chartered Accountants in Ireland. Each of these bodies has established Bye-Laws and Regulations with which their members are required to comply; in particular, the Bye-Laws include detailed requirements in relation to professional conduct and provide for a formal investigation and disciplinary process. Accordingly, members in the Isle of Man are regulated in precisely the same manner as members elsewhere in the British Isles.

There are 47 CIMA members on the Island with members located in the sectors of finance, tourism, transport, retailing and consultancy.

There are presently 108 ACCA members on the Island, 60 of whom are employed in industry and commerce, 27 are in public practice (of whom 12 hold ACCA practising certificates); 2 are employed in the public sector and 19 others have no business details. The 12 who hold ACCA issued practising certificates are monitored by ACCA's Practice Regulation Department in order to ensure that regulatory requirements are being met.

In addition, there are a small number of accountants who are members of the Chartered Institute of Public Finance and Accountancy.

With regard to professional conduct, all chartered accountants are bound by the mandatory requirements of their respective Institutes in relation to ethics and independence issues. These requirements address the very limited circumstances when an audit firm may undertake the provision of services to companies where the shareholders are trust entities in respect of which the firm provides trust/fiduciary services. Generally, chartered accountancy practices carrying on both audit and trust work are structured in one of two ways. Either all of the services provided are carried on through the chartered accountancy partnership or, alternatively, in the case of a number of firms, a separate trust company has been formed, the Directors of which would be the partners in the practice.

CHAPTER 13

CRIME PREVENTION

POLICIES AND STRUCTURES

13.1 Policy and International Agreements

The Island has a very clear commitment to prevent, deter and punish crime of all kinds, including tax offences, within the Island and is willing to assist other jurisdictions in the pursuit of criminals and crime to the greatest extent possible.

To that end, the Island has introduced an armoury of laws, regulations and enforcement practices similar to those of the United Kingdom, together with modern systems designed to maximise the chances of detection, prosecution and confiscation. The authorities collaborate with authorities in the United Kingdom and other jurisdictions regularly in pursuit of serious crime.

13.2 Prevention of Money Laundering

From the earliest days, Isle of Man Government has been committed to ensuring the Island offers no welcome to money launderers. The Anti-Money Laundering Guidance Notes, first issued in 1991, and 1992 for Investment Business and in 1996 for Insurance Business, were significant early steps in setting out the minimum standards expected of licenceholders.

In recent years, the Financial Action Task Force against money laundering formed by the main industrial nations (FATF) has increased international pressure to urge compliance within their 40 recommendations and the Isle of Man has a firm policy to support and comply with the 40 recommendations. The Treasury Minister has given a formal undertaking of support to the FATF on behalf of the Isle of Man Government.

In May, 1987, Tynwald passed the Drug Trafficking Offences Act. That Act was almost entirely based on the Drug Trafficking Offences Act 1986 (an Act of the Westminster Parliament) and the Criminal Justice Act 1991 extended the scope of the money laundering provisions of the 1987 Act.

The Prevention of Terrorism Act 1990 created offences of assisting in the retention or control of terrorist funds, whether by concealment, removal from the jurisdiction, transfer to nominees or otherwise.

The Drug Trafficking Act 1996 consolidated, with amendments, the Drug Trafficking Offences Act 1987. The Act was closely based on the Drug Trafficking Act 1994 (of the Westminster Parliament). It retained all the "laundering" offences and added new offences of failing to disclose knowledge or suspicion of the laundering of the proceeds of drug trafficking and of prejudicing drug money laundering investigations by "tipping-off". The same extensive powers for the Police and Customs Authorities to obtain information were repeated.

In July, 1993, the Westminster parliament passed new legislation to create offences in relation to the laundering of the proceeds of crimes other than drug trafficking. These new offences were very closely modelled on the money laundering offences contained in drug trafficking legislation. A Criminal Justice (Money Laundering Offences) Bill was introduced into the House of Keys in 1997. It has been enacted and came into effect on the 1st July, 1998. The new Act mirrors the money laundering offences contained in the United Kingdom Criminal Justice Act 1993 and the Island's anti-money laundering legislation is fully compatible with the FATF 40 recommendations.

A Police Powers and Procedures Act also passed into law this year. That Act gives the Police additional powers of entry, search and seizure in relation to serious arrestable offences. These are powers which will be available to assist in obtaining evidence and intelligence for criminal investigations and proceedings in both the Isle of Man and outside the Isle of Man. The statutory powers follow very closely provisions contained in the Police and Criminal Evidence Act 1984 (an Act of the Westminster parliament).

FATF-style Evaluation

In 1994, the Isle of Man's legislation and procedures for combatting money laundering were subjected, at the Island's own invitation, to a FATF-style evaluation by United Kingdom and Dutch officials of the FATF. The conclusions from this review were that:

> "49. The Isle of Man is in substantial compliance with the FATF Recommendations. Its legislation is effective, and following the passage of the new Criminal Justice Bill, it will be more so. Financial supervisors and financial institutions are aware of the threat posed by money laundering, and have taken action against it from a very early stage.
>
> 50. The limited experience that individual financial institutions have had of money laundering cases may limit the effectiveness of the legislation, but the new guidance notes will help address this. Closer discussions between the Financial Supervision Commission, the Fraud Squad and the financial institutions on individual cases would also improve the understanding of the problems posed by money laundering at the level of individual financial institutions."

[Note: The Criminal Justice Bill referred to in the conclusions was an earlier and less comprehensive version of the legislation subsequently enacted in 1998.]

A fresh evaluation under the auspices of the FATF in co-operation with the Offshore Group of Banking Supervisors is planned for late in 1998.

The Criminal Justice (Money Laundering Offences) Act 1998 is concerned primarily with the reporting of transactions and the confiscation of assets. It has created a number of new substantive offences in relation to the laundering of the proceeds of crime other than drug trafficking. As part of the scheme of the Act, defences are created in certain cases if a transaction is reported to the Police. The information contained in such a report, because of section 17G in Schedule 2 to that Act, is subject to a duty of confidence. The duty does not apply to information in the hands of the Police from any other source nor to suspicious transaction reports concerning drug trafficking. The restrictions in the proposed section 17G are based on provisions in the Financial Services Act 1986 (an Act of the Westminster parliament).

The Police will be able to disclose the information to which the restrictions apply to persons in the Island for criminal investigations purposes and on other grounds. Disclosure to persons outside the Island are permitted under section 17I with the consent of the Attorney General if the information is disclosed for the prevention or detection of crime or the institution of or otherwise for the purpose of criminal proceedings outside the Island. The Attorney General proposes to issue general consents which will permit the Police to pass the information to NCIS, etc., without individual specific consents from the Attorney General. This course of action is specifically permitted by Section 17I. The Island authorities are currently considering the provisions of a draft memorandum of understanding with NCIS on mutual co-operation.

It is emphasised that the requirement for the Attorney General's consent only applies in respect of information contained in a suspicious transaction report made for the purposes of the Criminal Justice (Money Laundering Offences) Act 1998. It does not apply to any other information in the hands of the Police.

One of the key tools in the fight against money laundering is education. The need to raise awareness of the problem and the legal requirements placed upon businesses and individuals is a high priority. Seminars and conferences on money laundering have been held on the Island over a period of several years at the instigation of various Island authorities. These have been targeted at accountants, banks, insurance companies and stockbrokers. Representatives of all the local law enforcement and regulatory bodies have given presentations and answered questions and given information on trends. Assistance has also been given to the Law Society, with Customs, Police officers and the Chief Executive of the Financial Supervision Commission giving presentations to a recent training seminar. These seminars will be repeated on a regular basis to keep the importance of the issue in the forefront of the minds of the industry and to cater for regular changes in personnel.

It is in the nature of things that data are not available on the quantities of money laundered in any jurisdiction. What can be said, however, is that the possibility of laundering money unnoticed "through" a bank in the Isle of Man where the banking industry is small and well regulated is much reduced compared to other larger jurisdictions.

13.3 Tax Offences

Indirect Taxation

The Customs and Excise Agreement with the United Kingdom provides both parties with benefits and enables a common customs and fiscal area to exist. There is full co-operation between the two Customs organisations to prevent abuse of the indirect tax and duty systems. Through the Agreement, the Island has access to the European Single Market and has increasingly developed investigation, intelligence and data links with the EU and its members.

The Investigation and Intelligence Unit deals with many tasks undertaken elsewhere by fraud investigation units, including investigation of drug money laundering, VAT fraud, excise fraud, customs fraud, obtaining evidence, restraining and confiscating assets, assistance to other jurisdictions and sanctions.

Financial investigators from the Fraud Squad and Customs and Excise meet weekly. There is liaison of a less formal nature with other areas of the Isle of Man Constabulary. These links are being reviewed with a view to improving them by the signing of a memorandum of understanding.

Direct Taxation

The Income Tax Acts provide for both civil and criminal offences. The pursuit of non-compliance, whilst the specific responsibility of a number of officers in the Income Tax Division who have been trained accordingly, also forms part of the duties of various other groups within the Division.

Whilst offences will normally be investigated by officers of the Division under the provisions of the Income Tax Acts, in serious fraud cases investigations will be undertaken jointly with the Fraud Squad. The Legal Officer (Fraud) in the Attorney General's Chambers provides legal advice in such cases and determines the legislation under which proceedings are to be brought.

The Island has a Double Taxation Agreement with the United Kingdom. Section 15.4 of this report deals with this subject.

13.4 Police

The Isle of Man Constabulary comprises 218 Police officers and 37 Civilian support staff. Historically, the Chief Constable has been appointed from outside of the force and approximately one third of the force has experience in other jurisdictions.

The Fraud Squad has a staff of 8 Police officers, 1 accountant and a Civilian office manager. It also has a dedicated advocate in the form of the legal officer (fraud) on the staff of the Attorney General's Chambers.

As well as the work of financial investigation, the Fraud Squad also investigates alleged financial crime. The Fraud Squad also maintains its own intelligence data base. It also handles all requests for assistance from other jurisdictions, whether or not they relate to fraud or financial matters.

The Police Force is regularly inspected by one of Her Majesty's Inspectors of Constabulary to ensure that it is an effective force meeting standards equal to those in the United Kingdom.

POLICE, CUSTOMS, FRAUD AND FINANCIAL INVESTIGATION UNITS

Police	
Chief Constable:	Mr. R.E.N. Oake
Staff:	218 (Constabulary) 37 (Civilian support)
Fraud Squad	
Head:	Inspector C. Daughen
Staff:	8 Police (Plus Accountant, Legal Officer and Office Manager)
Customs and Excise	
Head:	Mr. D.G. Maxwell
Staff:	44

CHAPTER 14

INTELLIGENCE

14.1 Access to Financial Information about Individuals and Companies

The Isle of Man has no banking secrecy or other confidentiality laws. There is, however, as in the United Kingdom, the common law duty of care in respect of confidentiality and a respect for privacy. There are also restrictions on the passage of information contained in section 24 of the Insurance Act 1986 and sections 22 to 24 of the Financial Supervision Act 1988, the Data Protection Act 1986 and sections 106 to 106B of the Income Tax Act 1970.

Notwithstanding these limitations, the various regulatory and enforcement agencies have powers equivalent to their counterparts in the United Kingdom to obtain financial information on individuals and companies.

Specifically, the Island has enacted legislation which erodes the common law rules of confidentiality, especially in cases where crime or money laundering are suspected, except with regard to legal professional privilege These specific powers are described in Section 15.1.

14.2 Underground Banking and Shell Banks

The Isle of Man has not so far experienced any significant problems of underground banking. There have, however, been a few occurrences of 'shell banking', e.g. banking being conducted without a licence, and these have been investigated and stopped by the Enforcement Division of the Financial Supervision Commission at the very earliest opportunity. As is described elsewhere, the Commission has a strong enforcement policy and immediately uses its powers to injunct the company's activity and petition the court to freeze assets. Additionally, the Commission has powers to wind up in the public interest and does not hesitate to put matters for consideration before the court.

14.3 Transaction Reporting by Banks and Others

The Island authorities collaborate closely with banks and others with a view to identifying crime of all kinds, including fraud, tax evasion and money laundering. Ongoing liaison is maintained as part of the regular consultation between the Island's regulators and industry representatives.

As in the United Kingdom, the Island has a system for suspicious transaction reporting by banks, other financial institutions, lawyers, accountants and companies and other professional practices and partnerships. The obligation to report such transactions is set out in the various legislation relating to the prevention of terrorism, drug trafficking and money laundering.

Institutions are obliged to have Money Laundering Reporting Officers and, where necessary, Prevention Officers.

Both the institutions concerned and individual staff have a duty of vigilance. If they do not comply, they are liable to substantial penalties. Knowingly assisting another to retain or conceal the proceeds of crime, or to transfer those proceeds to another jurisdiction, nominee, or otherwise, carries a maximum penalty on conviction of 14 years imprisonment.

The reports are submitted to, and processed by the Fraud Squad and a steady increase in the number of reports year by year indicates the increased awareness within the Island of the possibilities of international financial crime and the need to safeguard the Island against being used to rechannel the proceeds of that crime.

The whole area of financial disclosure is an important one, causing financial institutions (and in reality all businesses) the onerous task of deciding whether to report details of hitherto confidential financial transactions to the police. Legislation requiring such disclosure has meant that businesses have had to modify their philosophy in the area of client confidentiality, adopting a more questioning approach.

The system works well and Isle of Man businesses have shown a good understanding of the law and that they are committed to the fight against money laundering.

14.4 Unexplained Lifestyle

Unexplained lifestyle may be a factor to be taken into account as part of an intelligence gathering operation but cannot be the sole determinant of enforcement action. There is no regular and systematic scrutiny of the population to identify cases where lifestyle does not match apparent resources, but the authorities are able to take lifestyle into account as part of investigatory or intelligence gathering operations.

Provisions similar to those in the United Kingdom Proceeds of Crime Act are contained within a Criminal Justice Bill included within the Island's legislative programme.

14.5 Sharing of Intelligence

The sharing of information is dealt with fully in Section 15. Much of the comment applied to sharing information applies to the sharing of intelligence. The Island authorities are generally willing to share the intelligence they have with other jurisdictions in pursuit of serious crime.

Some financial disclosures are made to Customs officers. These disclosures are referred to the Fraud Squad as the central collation point, but they and any other disclosures made directly to the Fraud Squad may be investigated by Customs and Excise.

Officers of the Constabulary provide intelligence to both the D.H.S.S. and income tax officers concerning individuals who apparently live beyond their means.

The Constabulary is willing to share information and intelligence with regulatory bodies and law enforcement agencies world-wide (See table below). Locally, weekly meetings are held with Customs officers whilst information of mutual benefit is exchanged with regulators as and when necessary, which means frequently.

Statistics
(Intelligence Sharing with Other Jurisdictions)

	1996	*1997*	*1998 (to end June)*
Interpol requests	74	80	61
U.K. force requests	209	227	120
Foreign force requests	73	51	40
Crown dependencies	17	10	12
Visiting officers	66	85	67

Chapter 15

Investigation

15.1 Obtaining Information

A number of agencies of the Isle of Man Government have statutory powers to require or obtain information which may be of relevance to financial crimes. These powers are broadly comparable to those available to equivalent agencies in the United Kingdom.

(a) Attorney General

The Attorney General has powers under sections 24 and 25 of the Criminal Justice Act 1990 (an Act of Tynwald) to require information to be furnished and documents to be produced for the purposes of investigation into serious or complex fraud. When necessary, a search warrant can be granted by a Justice of the Peace in support of a requirement. The powers are used by the Attorney General, or can be delegated by him, to Police Officers, for the investigation of serious and complex fraud committed within the jurisdiction of the Isle of Man. The powers are based on those conferred on the Director of the Serious Fraud Office in London.

(b) The Police

In a significant number of cases, the Police are able to apply to a Justice of the Peace for a warrant for access to documents or information to assist in the investigation of crime. The provisions which are relevant for this purpose are:-

- Section 2 of the Prevention of Fraud (Investment) Act 1968 under which a constable may enter and obtain access to documents and information relating to breaches of restrictions on the distribution of investment circulars.
- Section 108 of the Copyright Act 1991 gives a constable access to evidence relating to offences concerning intellectual property rights.
- The Customs and Excise Management Act 1986 confers on constables similar powers of search etc to those exerciseable by officers of Customs and Excise under that Act.
- Section 28 of the Theft Act 1981 gives Police Officers powers to search for evidence or stolen goods.
- Section 13 of the Computer Security Act 1992 gives constables access to information relating to breaches of that Act.
- Schedule 2B of the Misuse of Drugs Act 1976 contains powers to enable constables and officers of Customs and Excise to stop, search and obtain information on ships suspected of being used for illicit traffic in narcotic drugs.
- Schedule 7 to the Prevention of Terrorism Act 1990 confers on the Police powers of access to information. Warrants issued in the UK to the British Intelligence Services are recognised and validated for purposes of Manx law.
- Part 4 of the Drug Trafficking Act 1996 confers powers on constables to obtain information about alleged drug trafficking offences and the proceeds of drug trafficking.
- The Police Powers and Procedures Act 1998 confers general statutory powers of entry, search and seizure in the case of serious offences. Those powers may also be used for the collection of

evidence in respect of crimes committed outside the Island.

- Section 22 of The Drug Trafficking Offences Act 1987 makes similar provision for Production Orders as the Drug Trafficking Act 1996 and the use of either Act is determined by the date of the offences being investigated.

(c) *Customs and Excise*

- Officers of Customs and Excise have powers of access to information conferred by the Customs and Excise Management Act 1986. The powers are exerciseable in relation to excise matters, imports and exports and are the same as those exerciseable in the United Kingdom by HM Customs and Excise.
- The Value Added Tax Act 1996 contains powers for Customs and Excise officers to gain access to information for the purpose of value added tax offences.
- The Police Powers and Procedures Act 1998 supplements the powers of officers of Customs and Excise (such as in obtaining search warrants for evidence of customs and excise offences) in the same manner as the Police and Criminal Evidence Act 1984 did in the United Kingdom.
- Customs and Excise have powers under the Drug Trafficking Act 1996 to obtain Access Orders etc. in relation to the proceeds of drug trafficking, and to have any such proceeds confiscated following conviction of a drug trafficking offence in either the Island, United Kingdom or any of a number of other specified countries. The power to seize money at ports is also available to the Police as well as to Customs Officers.
- There are also powers to seize and detain large amounts of cash carried by travellers entering or leaving the Island if the money is suspected as being connected with drug trafficking. The limit is set at £10,000 for administrative purposes in the Isle of Man to coincide with the level legally defined by Her Majesty's Customs and Excise.

(d) *Financial Supervision Commission*

The Financial Supervision Commission has comprehensive powers to obtain or require information from all categories of business which are licensable by the Commission, i.e.

— Banks and Deposit Taking Institutions

— Investment Businesses

— Collective Investment Schemes

— Fund Managers

— Building Societies.

The Commission may also obtain information from those suspected, on reasonable grounds, to be engaged in such business without licence. Additionally, it has power to obtain information from any third party, where it is believed that party has information relevant to any investigation - See 6.1 and 6.2.

(e) *Insurance and Pensions Authority*

The Insurance and Pensions Authority has extensive powers under the Insurance Act 1986 and the Insurance Intermediaries (General Business) Act 1996 to require information for the purpose of exercising its functions. The specific powers are contained in sections 21 and 22 of the Insurance Act 1986 and sections 7 and 8 of the Insurance Intermediaries (General Business) Act 1996.

The Insurance and Pensions Authority may also require the insurer's actuary, auditor, insurance manager or banker to provide the information if the insurer itself fails to provide it.

These powers may be exercised by the Insurance Supervisor or by any person appointed in writing by the Insurance and Pensions Authority

(f) Assessor of Income Tax

Except for the purpose of Manx tax the Assessor does not undertake criminal investigations. In cases where serious tax offences are suspected, investigation will be undertaken jointly by the Police and the Assessor's office. The Legal Officer (Fraud) in the Attorney General's Chambers provides legal advice in such cases.

In relation to direct taxation the Assessor of Income Tax has authority under the Income Tax Acts to require information from various sources, the most important of which are all persons, corporate or individual, liable to income tax on the Island, exempt or international companies and persons making taxable payments.

There is also the ability under provisions contained in Social Security legislation to obtain information from that Department.

The Income Tax authorities in the Island have only limited powers to enforce the production of information and do not have any general power to make searches. The only search provision is a specific one within the Income Tax (Instalment Payments) Act 1974 enabling access to be gained if there is reason to believe that evidence will be found on the premises to show that the terms of the Act have not been complied with. Where the premises relate to a private dwelling house a warrant has to be obtained from a Justice of the Peace.

(g) General

In the case of all offences, the Isle of Man authorities are able and willing to require the production of documents and information wherever the actual or suspected crimes were committed. There are powers of entry, search and seizure which support those powers. The new Police Powers and Procedures Act has given extra powers to the Police additional to those which have been exercisable by the Attorney General and the Police in respect of crimes in the past.

There are no cut-offs in fraud cases. The statutory powers apply to criminal offences in respect of fiscal matters in the same manner and to the same extent as the English legislation on which they are based.

The legislation requiring disclosure clearly sets out the requirements and penalties for breaches of the law. To date, there have been no prosecutions on the Island for such offences. More than half of the 1997 disclosures came from banks, with almost all of the rest emanating from Insurance Companies.

Applications may be made to the Courts for orders in respect of bankers' books under the Bankers' Books Evidence Act 1935. The Act is based on the Bankers' Books Evidence 1879 (an Act of the Westminster parliament).

15.2 Sharing Information Inside the Jurisdiction

There are some restrictions on the sharing of information between agencies of the Government (See Section 14.1). These restrictions notwithstanding, there are a number of instances where information can be shared.

Section 106 (A) of the Income Tax Act 1970 allows the Income Tax Division to disclose information to the Customs and Excise Division of Treasury to assist in the performance of the duties of the latter. To date there is no legal cover for the flow of information from Customs and Excise to Income Tax. Legislation will be introduced to rectify this matter.

There are also provisions in place which enable information to be exchanged between the Income Tax Division and the Department of Health and Social Security in relation to matters within the benefits legislation and income tax legislation.

Since 7th July 1997, with the approval by Tynwald of the Social Security Administration (Fraud) Act 1997 (Application) Order 1997, there has been legal cover for the exchange of information, in both directions, between Customs and Excise and the Department of Health and Social Security (DHSS). Section 122 of the applied Act allows Customs and Excise to disclose to the DHSS information for the purposes of prevention and detection of benefit fraud and for use in civil or criminal proceedings under certain, named Social Security laws. Section 122 (c) of the applied Act allows DHSS to disclose information to Customs and Excise for use in assisting the Collector or an officer in the performance of his duties.

The Application Order relating to the Social Security Administration (Fraud) Act 1997 also extends to the Income Tax Division.

There are formal quarterly meetings between the Fraud Squad and compliance staff from the insurance companies and banks. In May, 1998, a liaison group was formed with representatives from the Fraud Squad, Financial Supervision Commission, Insurance and Pensions Authority, and Customs and Excise. The group meets monthly to consider matters of mutual interest.

The Police actively share intelligence at the investigation level with financial industry regulators. There are also occasions where fraud squad and the regulators mount joint investigations.

So far as the Courts are concerned, any information disclosed during public sittings of Court would be made available to law enforcement, regulatory and Tax Departments, upon request.

Both on their own initiative and in response to requests, the Island's regulatory authorities can and do provide information and assistance to other on-Island and off-Island regulators in response to specific requests. Except where the information forms part of the public record, it is not available for random examination and exploration by those outside the office of the regulatory body holding the information.

15.3 Sharing Information with Other Jurisdictions

The Attorney General's powers under sections 24 and 25 of the Criminal Justice Act 1990 can be used to assist overseas authorities in cases involving serious or complex fraud, wherever committed.

The Attorney General has further powers under section 21 of the Criminal Justice Act 1991 to assist Courts, Tribunals and investigating authorities in other jurisdictions. Under this power the Attorney General may apply to a stipendiary magistrate to order the production of evidence relating to a criminal investigation or criminal proceedings in other countries. When necessary a search warrant may be issued. The provisions are based on the Criminal Justice (International Co-operation) Act 1990 (an Act of Parliament). The provisions of Section 21 are used on a frequent basis and evidence in relation to all types of criminal offence is obtained in this way.

Special arrangements are in place under the Customs and Excise Agreement 1979 to enable Isle of Man Authorities and the UK Authorities to assist each other in relation to VAT and customs and excise matters.

Subordinate legislation made in relation to value added tax and customs and excise enables reciprocal assistance to be given to Member States of the European Community.

Under the terms of the Customs and Excise Agreement 1979, given legal effect in the Island by Orders made under the Customs and Excise (Transfer of Functions) Act 1979 of Tynwald and the Isle of Man Act 1979 of Parliament, and the Value Added Tax (United Kingdom) Order 1996, the Island and UK are treated as one area for Customs, VAT and Excise Duty Purposes. This permits the free flow of information between the two jurisdictions in Customs, Excise and VAT matters including information relating to offences.

The Isle of Man regularly obtains and shares intelligence with authorities outside the jurisdiction. This is often done on a informal basis as a precursor to more formal applications under, for example, the Criminal Justice Act 1990 or the Criminal Justice Act 1991.

Banks and financial institutions now regularly make suspicious transaction reports to the Police. These reports are promptly relayed to criminal intelligence organisations such as NCIS. The majority of suspicious transaction reports dealt with at present relate to funds where there is thought to be a possibility that they derive from drug trafficking.

The Criminal Justice (Money Laundering Offences) Act creates a number of new substantive offences in relation to the laundering of proceeds of crime other than drug trafficking. As part of the scheme of that Act, defences are created in certain cases if a transaction is reported to the Police. The new Act is likely to cause an increase in the number of suspicious transaction reports. Intelligence derived from these reports will be passed to appropriate criminal intelligence agencies.

The general powers to provide evidence for use outside the Island which are contained in section 21 of the Criminal Justice Act 1991 have no cut off point nor any general limitation on the class of offences to which they apply. Certain additional requirements are imposed where the offence is a fiscal offence and proceedings have not yet been instituted. The Act enables assistance to be given in genuine criminal cases, including tax crime, but does not extend to speculative enquiries by foreign tax authorities relating to tax collection. The section copies the law contained in section 4 of the Criminal Justice (International Co-operation) Act 1990 (an Act of the Westminster parliament). Under the Police Powers and Procedures Act 1998, the Police are given powers of entry, search and seizure in cases of serious arrestable offences. The powers can be used for the collection of information in respect of crimes committed outside the Island.

The Island is able to, and does, co-operate fully with the United Kingdom and other Member States of the European Community in customs matters. European Community law on mutual assistance in customs matters applies to the Isle of Man. Formal Co-operation Agreements entered into by the European Community with third countries and which have the force of community law extended to the Isle of Man.

The Island has voluntarily adopted the provisions of EC Directives on the mutual exchange of information and mutual recovery of value added tax and excise duties as between Member States. In particular, the EC Regulation 515/97 on mutual assistance in customs matters also allows for the introduction of the Customs Information System (CIS) data base on customs matters, for on line information exchanged between EC member states.

The Island voluntarily adopted EC regulation 218/92, and other associated instruments, in 1993 to allow for the exchange of information on EC acquisitions and dispatches between member states involving Island based businesses. This enabled the Island to function as a part of the single market for VAT purposes with effect from 1st January 1993.

Island law on data protection, in the manner of the application of data protection principles to manual records, will require addressing before the derogation granted to the United Kingdom (and hence the Isle of Man) expires in 2002.

The Isle of Man Income Tax authorities have no general powers for the collection of information for the benefit of tax authorities in other jurisdictions. Information gathered for the purposes of criminal investigations and criminal proceedings in respect of fiscal matters are dealt with in accordance with the standard English rules of international law. In cases where information can be given in accordance with those rules, the information will be obtained by the Attorney General, Police etc in the same manner as any other criminal case.

Customs and Excise have access to HM Customs and Excise intelligence systems and also contribute to those systems. The Isle of Man is also an associate member of FFIN. The position of officers of Customs and Excise as "constables" for the purposes of money laundering legislation has been clarified, and the exchange of information between the Fraud Squad and Customs and Excise can take place freely.

The confidentiality and information exchanged through the disclosure system is considered to be of paramount importance and great care is taken by those involved to ensure that any such information is handled with sensitivity. All police officers involved in the system are fully aware of the importance of confidentiality.

Formal Requests to the Police for the obtaining of evidence for the benefit of other jurisdictions in 1997[1]

Class of Request	*Request Received*	*Assistance Given*	*Proceed-ings Pending*	*Assistance Refused*
Drugs	20	19	1	
Terrorism	1	1		
Fraud, Tax and other offences	55	18	32	5[2]

[1] No figures available for earlier years.

[2] None of these were tax cases.

Whilst the Island has regularly assisted with enquiries from other jurisdictions into serious crime, the Island's experience of seeking and obtaining information from other jurisdictions has been generally disappointing. The Island has few examples where other jurisdictions have proved as helpful and responsive to enquiries as the Island itself has been.

15.4 Mutual Legal Assistance Treaties and Double Taxation Arrangements

Mutual Legal Assistance Treaties

The Island has decided, as a matter of principle, that any country with which the United Kingdom has a bilateral agreement on drugs should be the subject of an order made by the Department of Home Affairs under the Drug Trafficking Offences (Designated Countries and Territories)(Amendment) Order and that, generally, the Island should seek to be included in the Treaty.

The Isle of Man Government has agreed to be involved in the following:

- The Agreement between the United Kingdom and the U.S. Government concerning the investigation of drug trafficking offences and the seizure and forfeiture of the proceeds of drug trafficking was extended to the Island in September, 1992.

- Treaty between United Kingdom and Government of Romania concerning the restraint and confiscation of the proceeds and instruments of crime - extension requested, May, 1995.

- Treaty between the United Kingdom and the Government of Thailand on mutual assistance in criminal matters - extension requested, January, 1995.

- Mutual Assistance agreements in relation to drug trafficking - extensions requested in respect of United Kingdom agreements with 25 various jurisdictions.

- Council of Europe Convention on Mutual Assistance in Criminal Matters, 1959 - extension requested.

- Agreement between United Kingdom and Government of India concerning the restraint and confiscation of the proceeds and instruments of crime and terrorist funds, 1990 - extension requested, January, 1990.
- Legal Proceedings Convention:
  - United Kingdom/Belgium, 1932 - extended January, 1984
  - United Kingdom/Iraq, 1935 - extended January, 1984
  - United Kingdom/Hungary, 1935 - extended January, 1984
  - United Kingdom/Yugoslavia, 1936 - extended June, 1984
  - United Kingdom/Switzerland, 1937 - extended June, 1981
  - United Kingdom/Netherlands, 1932, 1967 - extended April, 1977
  - United Kingdom/Romania, 1978 - extended June, 1978
- Investment promotion and protection agreements, extensions requested in respect of United Kingdom Agreements with 35 jurisdictions.

This list is sufficient to confirm the willingness of the Island to co-operate internationally in the safeguarding of international business and the pursuit of international crime.

Double Taxation Arrangements

The Island has only one major double taxation arrangement. This is with the United Kingdom and it dates from 1955. Under that Arrangement, the Island has the ability to exchange information with the United Kingdom for the prevention of fraud or the administration of statutory provisions against legal avoidance in relation to the taxes covered by the Order.

Regular exchanges do take place and the respective Revenue Authorities seek to provide early and comprehensive responses.

Being an early model, there are limitations on the provisions contained within the Arrangement. Informal discussions have taken place about the possibility of bringing it up to date.

Chapter 16

Judicial proceedings

The approach of the Island authorities is that crime should be prosecuted whenever it is identified and there is sufficient evidence and a realistic prospect of conviction and there are tried and tested procedures to assist other jurisdictions by providing evidence for use in proceedings and for bringing prosecutions in the Island.

16.1 Domestic legislation

The range of penalties available in the Criminal Courts of the Isle of Man is broadly comparable to those available for similar offences tried by the English Criminal Courts. The Isle of Man Courts normally follow the sentencing policy and guidelines set for Courts in England.

The Extradition Act 1989 (an Act of the Westminster parliament), and Orders in Council under that Act, extend to the Isle of Man as part of Manx law. The procedure for extradition of persons in the Isle of Man is entirely governed by that legislation. The operation of the Act in individual cases is subject to extradition treaties, conventions and arrangements entered into by the United Kingdom and which extend to the Isle of Man. Extradition proceedings take place before a Stipendiary Magistrate in London.

Where necessary, criminal proceedings are backed up with civil applications, for example, applications for restraint orders or injunctions. The range of remedies available in, and the right of access to, the High Court in the Isle of Man are the same as those available in England. There is no special impediment to actions against fraudsters, money launderers or others involved in financial crime.

Since May, 1987, drug trafficking legislation has included power for the restraint and confiscation of the proceeds of drug trafficking offences. In 1990, similar powers were conferred on the Courts in relation to terrorist funds and the proceeds of other offences, including tax crime, which are triable on information (equivalent to English indictable offences).

In all these cases, the Isle of Man's Authorities have power to trace, restrain and confiscate the funds in question. The current powers are contained in the Criminal Justice Act 1990, the Prevention of Terrorism Act 1990 and the Drug Trafficking Act 1996. The powers are available for use, and are used, to assist other jurisdictions. The provisions have the same effect as the equivalent legislation in force in England.

The power of confiscation under the Criminal Justice Act 1990 is, in effect, an "all crimes" power. The power applies to offences which are triable on information (whether or not they are exclusively so triable) and lesser offences if prescribed by subordinate legislation. The Act applies to the same range of offences as the Criminal Justice Act 1988 (an Act of Parliament). There is no special provision which excludes specific tax offences or any other criminal offence (e.g. false accounting) which might relate to taxes. The powers of confiscation under the 1990 Act are exercisable where the criminal proceeds are at least £10,000.

In the case of suspected drug offences, terrorism, and other offences which are triable on information, the Island's Authorities have power to trace, restrain and confiscate the proceeds of crime. These powers are conferred by the Criminal Justice Act 1990, the Prevention of Terrorism Act 1990 and the Drug Trafficking Act 1996. The powers are used to assist other jurisdictions and the provisions have the same effect as the equivalent legislation in force in England.

The Criminal Justice (Money Laundering Offences) Act will add substantive offences to the existing armoury available in the Isle of Man against money laundering (see Section 13.2). Further legislation dealing with the confiscation of the proceeds of crime is in the list of forthcoming Bills.

The powers of confiscation etc under the Criminal Justice Act 1990 apply in relation to offences to which Part 1 of that Act applies. Part 1 of the Act applies to offences triable on information (whether or not it is exclusively so triable) and lesser offences which are prescribed by Order made by the Department of Home Affairs. The wording of the definition has the same effect as that contained in section 71(9)(c) of the Criminal Justice Act 1988 (an Act of Parliament) with the "gloss" of the Interpretation Act 1978 (an Act of Parliament). No special provision excludes tax offences or other criminal offences (eg false accounting) which might relate to taxes.

The legislation, in particular that contained in the Drug Trafficking Act 1996 and the Criminal Justice Act 1990, contain criminal procedures and civil law procedures. Both are used and both are designed to work in tandem with Isle of Man insolvency legislation.

In some cases physical assets as opposed to monies are restrained.

The range of remedies available in, and rights of access to, the High Court in the Isle of Man are the same as those available in England. There is no special impediment to actions against fraudsters, money launderers and financial institutions.

16.2 Assistance to Overseas Authorities

The vast majority of cases involving the restraint or confiscation of assets arises as a result of requests from other countries. Between 1992 and 1996, seventeen cases involving drug trafficking resulted in an amount of £2,324,200 being restrained or confiscated. In 1997, there was one case in which the amount restrained or confiscated was £7,000. Occasionally, physical assets as opposed to money have been restrained but values cannot be given.

The Judgments (Reciprocal Enforcement)(Isle of Man) Act 1968 provides for the registration and enforcement of foreign (including United Kingdom) judgements in the Isle of Man. But, in accordance with internationally accepted principles, certain foreign judgments for taxes and the like are not enforceable under that legislation.

As an earnest of the Island's willingness to act in response to requests from other jurisdictions, there is a long-standing arrangement with the Home Office that international agreements for mutual assistance in tracing, restraining, charging and confiscating assets held by suspects or convicted criminals should normally be extended to the Isle of Man. As a result of this policy, the principal multi-lateral mutual assistance treaties have been extended to the Island. A number of bi-lateral agreements have also been extended although, because of the large number of these agreements, the Home Office and the Foreign and Commonwealth Office have agreed between themselves to deal with extension in stages. The absence of a bi-lateral agreement extending to the Isle of Man does not affect Manx law. It is the practice of the Isle of Man Authorities to apply statutory powers to all countries with which the United Kingdom has an agreement. Further information can be found in Section 15.4.

Chapter 17

Some particular cases

Savings and Investment Bank Limited (SIB)

In 1982, the SIB, registered and licensed in the Isle of Man, collapsed with debts of some £37 million. Liquidators subsequently paid out dividends to depositors amounting to approximately 29p in the £1.00 and the Isle of Man Government instituted a one-off scheme of ex gratia payments to depositors from public funds, based on the United Kingdom Depositor Protection Scheme of the day. The scheme was aimed at helping the smaller depositor particularly.

SIB was a seminal experience for the Island and much of the regulatory system now in place and proposed can trace its origins to the SIB and its aftermath.

There was an immediate external review commissioned, undertaken by Bank of England staff, the principal result of which was the establishment of the Financial Supervision Commission in 1983 (see Section 5.4 (a)). From this came, in turn, the Insurance Authority, now the Insurance and Pensions Authority in 1986 (see Section 5.4 (b)). These may be seen as the first wave of response to SIB.

It took a number of years for the formal investigations and legal processes consequent upon the collapse of the SIB to be completed and for further lessons to be drawn. But in April, 1992, the Council of Ministers laid before Tynwald a report on certain aspects of Company and Trust Law. This report was the end result of the post-SIB reviews and may be said to herald the second wave of response to SIB. It proposed, in particular, the regulation of companies and trusts. The current proposals for the regulation of corporate service providers is the first element in the implementation of these proposals. The further initiatives proposed for the regulation of companies and trusts will follow in due course and in accordance with the Council of Ministers' report.

Also directly attributable to SIB was the decision of the Isle of Man Government to introduce legislation for investor protection funded by levies on regulated institutions (see Section 5.5).

Bank of Credit and Commerce International (BCCI)

On 5th July, 1991, international regulatory action co-ordinated by the Bank of England led to the closure of the BCCI group. There was a branch of BCCI on the Island and, following the winding up of BCCI, payments to depositors of the Isle of Man branch have been the only calls on the Island's Depositors' Compensation Scheme.

Notwithstanding the activities of BCCI and its officers elsewhere in the world, there is no evidence from the investigations of the Island's authorities and those from elsewhere that the Isle of Man branch was anything other than properly run.

The high standard of regulation on the Island and the depositor protection arrangements have served to ensure that the Island has not been implicated in the more reprehensible aspects of BCCI's activities and has been seen to respond responsibly and sympathetically to the interests of depositors.

Mil-Tec Corporation Limited (Mil-Tec)

In late 1997, media reports linked British companies, including Mil-Tec registered in the Isle of Man, to the supply of arms, in contravention of the U.N. embargo, to Rwandan extremists in Zaire. The situation was the subject of a United Kingdom inter-departmental committee report. This revealed that, consequent upon failures in communication between two United Kingdom Government Departments, the necessary subordinate legislation had not been put in place and that there was a gap in controls.

Whilst the failure to apply the U.N. sanctions was not attributable to any failure on behalf of the Island authorities, there was significant adverse publicity and public reaction to the activities of the company which affected adversely the reputation of the Island.

The Mil-Tec incident and the public response has been material in strengthening the resolve of the Isle of Man Government to institute appropriate and effective regulatory arrangements in respect of Manx registered companies.

The Agip case

An employee of Agip (Africa) Limited (Agip) misappropriated money from Agip and diverted it to recipients of his own choosing through companies which were provided and managed by a firm of Accountants in the Isle of Man.

In the circumstances of the case, one Accountant and his employee were judged by the U.K. Courts to be liable as constructive trustees and the other Accountant, who played no part in the fraud, to be liable for the acts of his partner Accountant and the employee of his firm.

Annex

PRINCIPAL LEGISLATION RELATING TO FINANCIAL REGULATION, COMPANIES AND TRUSTS, CRIME, MONEY LAUNDERING AND FORTHCOMING LEGISLATION

FINANCIAL REGULATION

Insurance Act 1986

The Act provides for the regulation of insurance companies. Insurance business is not permitted unless a company is authorised by the Insurance and Pensions Authority or is authorised in a member State of the European Community and is the holder of a permit issued by the authority. Insurers must maintain proper solvency and accounting standards. The Authority has powers require information, to carry out investigations and to wind up insurers.

Building Societies Act 1986

Under the Act building societies cannot accept deposits or subscriptions for their shares nor can they make loans or advances unless the society is authorised by the Financial Supervision Commission. The Act contains powers for the Commission to require information about the affairs of a building society.

Financial Supervision Act 1988

Collective investment schemes are regulated under this Act. Only schemes which are authorised or recognised by the Financial Supervision Commission may be promoted in or from the Island. Subordinate legislation regulates the constitution, solvency and administration of collective investment schemes.

Enabling powers under the Act have been exercised to make compensation schemes for participants in collective investment schemes and policyholders.

Investment Business Act 1991

Investment business is regulated and supervised by the Financial Supervision Commission under this Act. Only permitted persons may carry on investment business. The Commission has powers to require information, investigate the affairs of investment businesses and to issue enforceable directions to those carrying on investment business. Subordinate legislation provides specific rules as to the conduct of investment business.

Moneylenders Act 1991

The Act provides for the regulation of persons carrying on the business of money lending. Moneylending cannot be carried on unless the business is registered with the Board of Consumer Affairs. The Board has powers to obtain evidence of infringements by means of search warrants.

Credit Unions Act 1992

The Act regulates the establishment, registration and operation of credit unions and the Financial Supervision Commission is responsible for their supervision. The Commission has powers to require information, to suspend the operations of credit unions and to issue enforceable directions to credit unions.

Timeshare Act 1997

This Act provides for the regulation of timeshare agreements and timeshare credit agreements where there is some connection with the Isle of Man. The Act requires safeguards to be included in timeshare contracts and imposes a "cooling off" period. Enforcement is undertaken by the Board of Consumer Affairs.

Subordinate legislation provides detailed rules as to the carrying on of timeshare business.

Banking Act 1998

This Act consolidates existing legislation and adds improved enforcement powers. Banking business may not be carried on in or from within the Isle of Man without a licence granted by the Financial Supervision Commission. Licence-holders are required to be fit and proper.

The Commission has powers to obtain information, investigate the affairs of banks and issue enforceable directions to banks.

A scheme of compensation for depositors has effect under the Act.

COMPANIES AND TRUSTS

Companies Act 1931

The Companies Act 1931 provides for the incorporation of companies in the Isle of Man. The Act is based on the Companies Act 1929 (of the Westminster Parliament) but is much amended to reflect changes in commercial practices and regulatory needs.

The Act gives the High Court the power to appoint inspectors to investigate the affairs of companies. The inspectors report back to the High Court.

Trustee Act 1961

This Act is based on the Trustee Act 1925 of Parliament. Part I of the Act regulates the investment powers of trustees. Part II deals with the general powers of trustees, the delegation of powers by trustees and protective trusts. Part III regulates the appointment and discharge of trustees. Part IV provides for the powers of the court to appoint trustees and for vesting of trust property in trustees and the powers of the court to deal with trust property.

The Act is supplemented by legislation relating to the variation of trusts charitable trusts and the governing law of trusts.

Companies Act 1968

This Act updated the system of prospectuses for public offers.

Companies Act 1974

The Act made a number of amendments to the Companies Act 1931. It enables the Treasury to apply to the High Court for the appointment of inspectors in the public interest or where the company has been used for an unlawful purpose or persons concerned in its formation or management have been involved in misconduct. The Act also prohibited corporate directors.

Companies Act 1982

The principal effect of the Act was to update the accounting requirements of the 1931 Act. In addition new requirements were made for the appointment of directors and secretaries.

The Act enables the High Court to order that the directors of an insolvent company shall not be directors of, or involved in the management of, any company. Disqualification can last for 5 years.

Companies Act 1986

The principal effect of this Act was to permit companies to undertake any legal business without the need for the extensive recital of objects in a memorandum of association. The Act largely abolished the *ultra vires* rule for companies.

Companies Act 1992

The Act made extensive amendments to the existing law in the field of mergers and reconstructions, financial assistance by a company for the purchase of its own shares, the purchase by a company of its own shares, registry practice, administration of companies and private companies.

Power is also given to the High Court to order that an unfit individual shall not be a director, secretary, liquidator, receiver or manager of a company or to be involved in the promotion, formation or management of a company for 3 to 15 years. The grounds for making an order include - conviction for dishonesty (anywhere), conviction of 3 offences under the Companies Acts or similar overseas legislation, conviction of an offence relating to regulation of the financial services industry (anywhere), or failure to comply with certain orders of the High Court. Disqualification can be imposed for periods from 3 to 15 years.

Recognition of Trusts Act 1988

This Act implements the Hague Convention on the recognition of trusts.

Single Member Companies Act 1993

This Act enabled the establishment of companies having one member. Until 1993 the minimum number of members that a company could have was two. The Act made specific modifications to the Companies Act 1931 for the purpose.

Purpose Trusts Act 1996

This Act permits the establishment of trusts for a specific purpose rather than for the benefit of a particular beneficiary.

Companies (Transfer of Domicile) Act 1998

Part I of the Act enables foreign companies to re-establish in the Isle of Man as if they were companies incorporated in the Isle of Man under the Companies Acts 1931 to 1993. Such companies will, after re-establishing, be treated for all purposes as the same as Isle of Man incorporated companies.

Part 2 of the Act permits companies incorporated in the Isle of Man under the Companies Acts 1931 to 1993 to re-establish in other jurisdictions.

Limited Liability Companies Act 1996

The Act provides for the establishment, registration, accounts, administration and winding up of a new form of association called a limited liability company. The form is based on a concept which is well known in the United States of America. It embodies principles from both partnership and company law. The liability of the organisation is limited and operates in a similar manner to a body corporate but in other respects it resembles a partnership, for example it is tax transparent (the members are liable for taxes on the income of the company).

CRIMINAL LEGISLATION

Criminal Code 1872

This Act includes the offence of conspiracy to cheat and defraud.

Bankers' Books Evidence Act 1935

This Act enables a court to require a bank to allow a party to any civil or criminal proceedings to inspect and take copies of a banker's records.

Misuse of Drugs Act 1976

The sale, supply, import, production, etc. of restricted drugs are controlled under this Act in the same way as in the United Kingdom. In particular offences are created which apply to ships registered in the Isle of Man and foreign ships. The Act contains powers for constables, customs officers and other authorised persons to stop and search ships.

Criminal Law Act 1981

This extensive Act includes powers for criminal courts to deprive convicted persons of property used or intended for use for the purposes of crime. Section 32 of the Criminal Justice Act 1991 extends the power to enable assistance to be given for the enforcement of similar orders in other countries.

Corruption Act 1986

This Act creates offences in relation to corrupt transactions and includes transactions by Isle of Man residents while outside the Island. There is a rebuttable presumption that gifts, etc to members and servants of public bodies are corrupt.

Summary Jurisdiction Act 1989

This Act governs the operation of courts of summary jurisdiction in the Isle of Man. It includes powers for the police in the Island to execute warrants issued in UK or Channel Islands. The power applies to warrants of arrest or commitment issued by courts, judges and magistrates.

Prevention of Terrorism Act 1990

The Act closely follows the United Kingdom legislation on the subject. Part 3 makes it an offence to give financial assistance for terrorism, to certain terrorist organisations and to assist in the retention of terrorist funds.

The Act contains detailed powers in relation to the investigation of terrorist activities and organisations and the tracing and seizure of terrorist funds. Enables a police constable to obtain access to material which is relevant to a terrorist investigation under an order made by a judge. It is an offence to fail to pass to the police information about suspected acts of terrorism.

Criminal Justice Act 1990

Part 1 (Sections. 1 - 22) : Enables a criminal court in the Isle of Man to order the confiscation of the proceeds of crime. The power is exercisable when a person is convicted of certain criminal offences. There are also powers to restrain the proceeds of crime pending the making of a confiscation order. The powers may be used to assist overseas authorities.

Part 2 (Sections. 24 - 25) : Confers on the Attorney General for the Isle of Man the power to require any person to provide information in relation to serious or complex fraud. The power is available to assist overseas authorities.

Criminal Justice Act 1991

This Act includes procedures for obtaining information, documents and evidence for use by courts and investigating authorities outside the Isle of Man. The information is obtained before a court on the application of the Attorney General.

Rules are provided for the service of external process in the Isle of Man and the Act also allows the Isle of Man to provide assistance in the enforcement of forfeiture orders made by overseas courts in respect of the modalities of crime.

Drug Trafficking Act 1996

This Act follows very closely the Drug Trafficking Act 1994 (an Act of the Westminster Parliament).

It enables a criminal court in the Isle of Man to order the confiscation of the proceeds of drug trafficking. The power is exercisable when a person is convicted of a drug trafficking offence. Powers are included to trace and restrain the proceeds of drug trafficking pending the making of a confiscation order. The powers may be used to assist overseas authorities.

The police and to customs and excise officers are given powers to seize cash which is being imported or exported and which is believed to be the proceeds of drug trafficking.

The Act also contains a number of offences relating to the laundering of the proceeds of drug trafficking.

Police Powers and Procedures Act 1998

The Act is based on the Police and Criminal Evidence Act 1984 (an Act of the Westminster

Parliament). It deals with a broad range of police powers but includes provisions for the issue of search warrants to the Police to obtain information and to seize articles. The powers can be used to obtain evidence in respect of crimes committed inside and outside the Isle of Man.

Criminal Justice (Money Laundering) Act 1998

The Act amends the Prevention of Terrorism Act 1990 and the Criminal Justice Act 1990 to bring offences relating to the laundering of terrorist funds and the proceeds of crime into line with the provisions currently in force in the United Kingdom.

New offences relating to "all crimes" money laundering are created and powers are conferred to make anti-money laundering codes which will set down rules as to the systems, training and business practices to put in place by businesses which handle money.

Insider Dealing Act 1998

This Act creates offences relating to the misuse of *inside* price sensitive information and replaces the Company Securities (Insider Dealing) Act 1987. The Act provides powers for the Treasury to appoint inspectors to investigate cases of suspected insider dealing. The inspectors report to the Treasury and have powers similar to those conferred on inspectors appointed under the Companies Acts to investigate the affairs of companies. The Treasury may publish the reports or evidence contained in them.

INSOLVENCY

Bankruptcy Code 1892

This Act establishes the substantive rules for the bankruptcy of individuals. Part I sets out the nature of acts of bankruptcy and the consequences of an adjudication of bankruptcy. Part II describes the disqualifications to which a bankrupt is subject. Part III deals with the administration of the property of a bankrupt, the effect of the bankruptcy on antecedent transactions. Part IV provides for trustees in bankruptcy, the trustee's accounts and the release of the trustee. The Act also deals with deeds of arrangement and fraudulent debtors.

Bankruptcy Procedure Act 1892

This Act provides the rules for the regulation of court practice and procedure in bankruptcy and associated matters.

Companies Act 1931

Part V deals with the liquidation and winding up of companies. The Act sets out the modes of winding up (i.e. by the court, voluntary or subject to the supervision of the court). Compulsory winding up is usually undertaken where the company is unable to pay its debts but also arises where the court is satisfied that it is just and equitable or where it is in the public interest.

The Act provides for the appointment and regulation of liquidators, the powers of the court, the liquidation of the companies assets, payments to creditors, priorities and the dissolution of companies.

Bankruptcy Act 1988

This Act confers statutory powers on the High Court to assist bankruptcy courts from other jurisdictions.

PROPOSALS FOR LEGISLATION IN 1998/99

Anti-Money Laundering Code

A draft code has been prepared under the enabling powers conferred by the Criminal Justice (Money Laundering Offences) Act 1998. The draft sets out anti-money laundering measures to be taken by businesses to recognise and prevent money laundering. The Code will apply to a wide variety of businesses such as banks, insurers, building societies, *bureaux de change*, casinos, lending institutions, professionals, etc. It is expected to come into operation on 1 October 1998.

Corporate Service Providers Bill

Proposals for legislation to licence and regulate corporate service providers [e.g. company formation agents and those providing professional company secretary services] are currently subject to public consultation. A Bill is expected to be introduced early in the 1998/99 session.

Insolvency Bill

This project will revise the current law relating to the winding up of the affairs of insolvent companies. The proposals are likely to result in new law relating to corporate rescue, updating of current law and procedures and the introduction of new provisions giving a more proactive role to the office of Official Receiver. This Bill is included in the current 1998/99 session programme.

Pensions Bill

This Bill is in the process of drafting. It will provide a system for the authorisation of pensions schemes on a similar basis to the system in place for collective investment schemes. The enforcement authority will be the Insurance and Pensions Authority which will have extensive investigation and enforcement powers.

Printed in the UK for The Stationery Office Limited on behalf of the Controller of Her Majesty's Stationery Office
Dd 5068441 11/98 65536 Job No 64716 45/44802